George Seymour Hollings

The Life of the Counsels

Short Instructions on Evangelical Perfection

George Seymour Hollings

The Life of the Counsels
Short Instructions on Evangelical Perfection

ISBN/EAN: 9783337054809

Printed in Europe, USA, Canada, Australia, Japan

Cover: Foto ©Lupo / pixelio.de

More available books at **www.hansebooks.com**

THE
LIFE OF THE COUNSELS.

SHORT INSTRUCTIONS

ON

EVANGELICAL PERFECTION.

By C. S. H.

With a Preface by the Rev. G. S. HOLLINGS, *Chaplain General to the Sisters of Bethany.*

"Be ye separate, saith the Lord."

LONDON:
W. KNOTT, 26, BROOKE STREET, HOLBORN.
1890.

TO HIM

WHO HATH CHOSEN US

AND RECEIVED US UNTO HIMSELF

AND

WHO HATH BOUND US WITH A THREEFOLD CORD

WHICH IS NOT QUICKLY BROKEN

THAT

AS HE IS SO WE SHOULD BE IN THIS WORLD

RICH THROUGH HIS POVERTY

PURE WITH HIS CHASTITY

PERFECT IN HIS OBEDIENCE.

PREFACE.

The following series of Letters upon the pursuit of the life of conformity to the Evangelical Counsels outside the cloister, appears to me to meet a very real need. They bear upon their face the evidence of having been written by one who speaks that which she knows, and testifies to that of which she has had prolonged experience.

The sound sense which pervades this little work will, I am sure, be thankfully recognized by all who are in the least familiar with the dangers which beset those who seek to lead the life of which it treats. And if its tone should appear in some passages rather foreign than English, that may be, at least in part, attributable to the fact that any soul impelled by God the Holy Ghost to a life of Evangelical Perfection can find but little help in recent English theology; so that what Jeremy Taylor complained of as to "books of casuistical theology" is true to-day of works on the Life of the Counsels, that we are "almost wholly unprovided," and that we "receive our answers from abroad."*

The general principles of the life of the Evangelical Counsels must be regarded as immutably true, since they are based upon an interpretation of Holy Scripture which bears the test of the Vincentian Canon; but there is doubtless in their application much which belongs to the field of debateable opinion. The recognition of the estate

* Preface to "Ductor Dubitantium."

of Religion is, for all Catholics, removed from the arena of controversy, by the imprimatur which has been generally accorded to it by the universal Church, and by her legislating for those called to its observance; whilst, at the same time, the relation in which that phase of the regenerate life stands towards the Episcopate is as clearly set forth in the Canons of Chalcedon.

Written as these Letters have been at the desire of the Author's spiritual guide, his commendation would have, perhaps, been their more fitting introduction, and must in any case have carried more weight with English Catholics than any words of mine; but I have been asked to write a brief Preface, and shall be thankful if by complying with the request I may in the least degree further a faithful effort to help those who are seeking, in the practise of the

Counsels of Evangelical Perfection, to follow that dear and adorable Lord, Whose "Name" to such is indeed "as ointment poured forth."

GEORGE SEYMOUR HOLLINGS.

Ascension Day, 1890.

CONTENTS.

LETTER	PAGE
I. Of what is meant by Evangelical Perfection	1
II. Of Vocation	10
III. Of the Religious and the Secular States	25
IV. Of Evangelical Poverty	49
V. Of Evangelical Poverty (2)	60
VI. Of the Rewards of Evangelical Poverty	71
VII. Of Evangelical Chastity, and of the Excellence of Holy Virginity	83
VIII. Of the Virginal Sacrifice	98
IX. Of the Virginal Sacrifice (2)	116
X. Of the Joys of Holy Virginity	128
XI. Of the Beauty of Holy Virginity	147
XII. Of the Reward of Holy Virginity	157
XIII. Of the Counsel of Evangelical Obedience	169
XIV. Of Spiritual Direction	184
XV. Of Religious Obedience	201
XVI. Of Vows, and of the Dedicated Life in the World	211
XVII. Of Special Devotions	234
A Rule of Life	249

ERRATA.

P. 39, line 9. — *After* " means " *insert* " the condition of."

P: 72, line 7 from bottom.—*For* " against " *read* " in respect to."

P. 105, line 14 from bottom.—" Elias . . availing " *read as quotation.*

THE LIFE OF THE COUNSELS.

LETTER I.

Of what is meant by Evangelical Perfection.

I HAVE been asked, dearest sisters, to write something that may help you to understand better the Counsels of that life of Evangelical Perfection, to which, as we have reason to believe, it has pleased our Lord to call us. It will be easiest for me, and I think also it will be agreeable to you, that these instructions should take the form of letters. I have already spoken to some of you from time to time on this subject, so this little book will only be a kind of supplement to what has gone before.

For the sake of others, however, to whom the subject is perhaps new, and for ourselves also, who continually need to be reminded even of things which we already know, let us begin at the very beginning, and ask, What is meant by Evangelical Perfection?

You remember the beautiful Gospel story of the young man (*St. Matt.* xix. 16; *St. Mark* x. 17), who came to Jesus, saying, "Master, what shall I do to inherit eternal life?" The answer to this question was, "If thou wilt enter into life, keep the commandments." The young man answered Him, "All these have I kept from my youth up, what lack I yet?" Then Jesus beholding him, loved him, and said to him, "One thing thou lackest: go thy way, sell whatsoever thou hast, and give to the poor, and thou shalt have treasure in heaven; and come, take up the cross, and follow Me."

Two very different questions were asked by this young man, and two very distinct answers were given. The meaning of the first question was, "What must I do to be saved?" and of the second, "What must I do to be perfect?"

The meaning of the first answer was, "Do your duty to God and to your neighbour, as Moses commanded;" and of the second, "Part with everything you have, and then come of your own free will, and follow Me in obedience unto death." The young man, you see, was not satisfied with the mere keeping of the commandments; he felt that he lacked something; yet he could truly say that he had always kept the commandments, and he had Christ's own assurance that no more than this was necessary to eternal life. "What lack I yet?" he said, and something about him touched the human Heart of Jesus, and moved Him to love the young man with a special love. He himself did not know what he wanted, but Jesus knew; he wanted to be perfect.

But the conditions of perfection were hard, too hard for the young man's zeal and courage at that time. He went away sorrowful, for he had great possessions. The disciples themselves were exceedingly amazed at the severity of these conditions, and were disposed to murmur at it; yet our Lord made no concessions, but only reiterated what He had already said.

I think, my sisters, we should do very well to bear this in mind. Evangelical Perfection is so difficult a thing that Christ Himself says of it, "With man it is impossible," although He adds for our comfort

"But not with God, for with God all things are possible." The way of the counsels, as it is called (to distinguish it from the ordinary Christian life, which is the way of the commandments), is a life of voluntary mortification, of perpetual self-oblation. It is a slow martyrdom, a death by inches; not a painless unconscious sort of death, but a generous, heroic, glad self-sacrifice.

Evangelical Perfection sets at nought the maxims of the world—not in theory only, for all Christianity does that—but in vigorous daily practice, which some Christianity certainly does not. The world says, "Be religious if you like, but do not altogether break with me. I can find you useful work to do, and harmless pleasures to enjoy, and innocent ways of making money, and agreeable friends, and a fair reputation. Be as philanthropic as you like, do all the good to others that you can, but do not forget that you owe certain duties to yourself. Above all things avoid singularity, and beware of foolishness." This is the language of the world, and with too many Christians it gets a hearing.

But the spirit of Evangelical Perfection is something very different from this. It turns its back upon the world altogether, and sets its face towards God. It shares His tastes, studies His choices, and makes them its own. It sets before itself the standard of Jesus Crucified, and measures itself by that. It is content to be counted foolish for Christ's sake, for it knows that the foolishness of God is wiser than the world. It hears Jesus saying, "Sell whatsoever thou hast," and it becomes poor for His sake ; it hears Him saying, "There be some that have made themselves eunuchs for the kingdom of heaven's sake," and its love is equal to the virgin sacrifice; it hears Him saying, "Take up thy cross and follow Me," and it yields itself in obedience unto death for Him.

Let us ask ourselves, sisters, if this is what we mean to face in our own life? Do not let us deceive ourselves. Evangelical Perfection can only be arrived at in this way, and unless we make up our minds to suffering we shall never be able to reach it. It often amazes me to hear the light manner in which some people talk of "perfection," as if it were a mere additional ornament to every-day Christianity, which can be made to wear the look of the world so well that it is hardly distinguishable from it. With what degree of truth can one who, as innocently as possible, enjoys all the gaieties of a London season, say, "I am crucified with Christ?" What to such a person do these words mean, "The world is crucified unto me, and I unto the world?" I speak of those who really find pleasure in such things, not of others to whom a total renunciation of them might be an impossibility. At least, my sisters, be assured that to us, who aim at Evangelical Perfection, these expressions must be stern and positive experiences. The world must indeed be crucified unto us, and we unto the world, and we must be "crucified with Christ," on a cross, on Calvary, in spiritual nakedness, in desolation, in darkness, and—save that we are with Christ—alone.

Now the very fact that this is of "counsel" and not of commandment will be an argument against it in the minds of many. Why undertake responsibilities which incur so much pain, when they are not absolutely necessary? If keeping the commandments can secure for us eternal life, why labour to observe the Counsels? If it is so easy to be saved, why not be content with salvation? Perfection is difficult; with men it is impossible; and since it is not strictly speaking necessary, would it not be better to take a lower standard, less glorious indeed, but more secure?

These are questions which we shall presently have to consider; but we know beforehand that with God all things are possible, and we feel, like the young man in the Gospel, that we "lack something." I am afraid that we should hardly dare to say that we have kept all the commandments from our youth up; but perhaps we are trying to keep them now, and God has blessed our efforts, and is making us long for something higher and better. We have caught sight of the Son of Man Who had not where to lay His head; and the poverty of Jesus has spoken to us from the manger and from the Cross, and has put us to shame. We look at our own life, and we feel that we lack something. We may not have "great possessions," but we have some, and He possesses nothing. Every day, while striving more and more to keep the commandments, and being, by God's mercy, preserved perhaps from mortal sin, we are conscious of what seems a growing unlikeness between ourselves and Jesus Christ. It is not so really, but it seems so. We begin to feel that keeping the commandments only is not enough, we want to be doing something more. The foolishness of the Cross begins to attract us; we do not want to bear it only by compulsion, we want to take it up and carry it, of our own free choice. And we do not want to remain where we are; everything about us is pleasant enough, and we are on the whole free to do our will in many things: but somehow it is not our own will that we want to be doing. We hear a voice saying, "Follow Me," and we look up and behold the Lamb of God; His face is set towards Calvary, and we see that He is going to be sacrificed; and as He passes us He looks into our face, and we know that He loves us with a special love, and the one thing that we lack becomes clear to us—we want to be perfect with the perfection of Jesus.

You, my sisters, will understand what I mean. The day when this happened to us is a day in our life to be remembered. Those for whom it is yet to come will understand, too, in their turn. It is only the beginning, but what a difference between all that follows and all that went before! This is a time to pray, and keep silence, and wait for the leadings of God. But chiefly it is a time to be humble. All that has happened to us as yet is, that we have realized what our lack is, and that if we would be perfect we must follow Christ as we have never followed Him before. But where or how we are to follow Him is not yet plain; only we know that it means suffering, and suffering so real that the young man whom Jesus loved went away sorrowful, not having courage to face it. This may be the case with some of us, dear sisters, for that young man is not the only one who has failed of his call. Many strive to enter into this way, and cannot. Let us be humble, and remember that we can of our own selves do nothing. Let us be very courageous too, for God's grace is sufficient for us, and His strength is made perfect in weakness. To Him be praise for ever.

LETTER II.

Of Vocation.

I THINK, my sisters, that what we have already said about the difficulty of Evangelical Perfection, and also that it is "of counsel" and not of commandment, should be enough to make us see that we should not enter rashly into this way, nor indeed should we take it upon *ourselves* to enter into it at all. No man goeth a warfare at his own cost, and if we undertake any great enterprise we ought first of all to consider whether we are really called to it, and if we are not, then it is the part of wisdom, as well as of humility, not to make the attempt. So before entering the way of Evangelical Perfection we must make sure as far as we can that God has given us the call: in other words we must feel that we "have a vocation."

Vocation means "call," and it is clear that no one can call himself. It is something which comes to us from without, from God; it is His voice speaking to the soul, and telling the soul what He means that it should do. We know that our God had a purpose in making us, and that purpose was His glory. He made us for a special object, to do some particular work for Him, and He desires that we should fulfil the end for which we were made, and do just what He means us to do, and nothing else. Some He calls to be apostles; it is their vocation to go out into the world and bring men to Christ. Some He calls to be evangelists; it is their vocation by word and work to pourtray Christ to men. Some He calls to be martyrs; and their blood is the seed of the Church. Some are called to be prophets; and the Holy Spirit uses them as His mouthpiece to teach divine mysteries. Some are called to be virgins; and they are to follow Jesus in a special way of their own, and not to set their love upon any creature, but to care only for the things of the Lord. All these are different vocations, and as the Lord hath called everyone, so let him walk. No one calleth himself, but is called of God.

There is a vocation which is common to all Christians; it is the vocation to holiness. All are called to be saints, and yet how rare holiness is! But it is necessary; for without holiness no man can see God. The faithful keeping of the commandments ensures holiness; but Evangelical Perfection is something more than this. Are we right, my sisters, in aiming so high? Do our present attainments warrant it? Is it not, after all, perhaps mere presumption? Should we not do well to content ourselves with what is necessary, and walk humbly in the more common way, and not put out our hand to high things? It would be safer, surely, and would it not be also really better? Who are we, that we should seek great things for ourselves, when others far worthier of them are satisfied with what is lowly?

This is very true, and would be quite unanswerable, if the desire for perfection were all our own. It is certain that we are not worthy of the least of God's gifts, and that we cannot, without rashness, of ourselves seek for great ones. But let us remember that the potter hath power over the clay, and of the same lump can fashion one vessel to honour, and another to common use. If it has pleased God to create us vessels of honour to Himself, let us give glory to Him, and not, through a false humility, fail of our vocation. After all, when we remember what God's choices are, and that He chooses the "foolish things," and the "weak things," and the "base things," we see that it is because of our extreme worthlessness that He has chosen us, just because we are foolish, weak, and base ; and if this be so, there is nothing to be proud of, I think. God gets most glory for Himself out of such as we are, precisely for this reason, that His strength is made perfect in weakness. Besides, after all, it is only a matter of obedience. To the soul that is called in this way, the "counsels" become as "commandments." If we so much as look back, we are not fit for the kingdom of God.

But you ask, What constitutes vocation? and how shall we know if we really are being called to this perfection? How are we to distinguish between our own mere desire and a divine call?

Divine vocations are given in two different ways, ordinarily and extraordinarily. St. Paul's vocation was extraordinary ; it came suddenly, visibly, and audibly : not only Saul himself, but those who were with him knew that something miraculous had happened. The vocation of David came in a less extraordinary way. "God chose David

His servant, and took him from the sheepfolds: from following the ewes great with young He brought him to feed Jacob his people, and Israel his inheritance." (*Ps.* lxxviii. 70.) The prophet Samuel was sent to tell David of the future which was in store for him; and he "anointed him with oil in the midst of his brethren, and the Spirit of the Lord came upon David *from that day forward*" (1 *Sam.* xvi. 13), but he was not raised to the kingdom till some years later. It was a vocation which came by degrees, and had to be developed and matured by the gradual workings of the Holy Spirit within his soul, and by all kinds of external troubles and persecutions.

But neither of these vocations are types of what we are to look for in ourselves. They are both, in different degrees, extraordinary *in kind*. We are not to expect either a voice directly from heaven, nor the voice of a heaven-sent teacher, to come to us as to St. Paul and to David. God generally speaks in ordinary ways. He comes to us in the common experiences of life, and speaks without form of words, yet very unmistakeably, to our souls. A conviction forces itself upon us that God wants us to do something for Him, or that He requires us to be different from what we are. Perhaps we are puzzled, we hardly know how to express what we feel, only we are conscious that something has spoken within us, and that the voice is not our own, but that of another. What the voice means, what it says, what it is calling us to do, we could not always say; only we know that our heart is burning within us as it never burned before, and we remember that Jesus said that He came to send fire on the earth.

The voice haunts us, and it fascinates us too. It grows more importunate, it leaves us no rest. We hear it as we wake in the morning, and it is still calling when we go to bed at night; it has been calling all the day. We are wearied with trying to understand it, and failing to catch the words; yet we would not for anything be without it. We are in suspense, which of course means that we are in pain, but there is a mysterious happiness in this pain which is quite unlike anything we have known before. We feel that we cannot bear it much longer, but time goes on, and we find that we are bearing it still; only we are suffering more than we were awhile ago, and we wonder if this will ever end, and how.

Now, dear sisters, this is clearly a state of things which we have not brought about of ourselves. No excited imagination, no morbid fancies of our own, could possibly effect this; for see, here is suffering which is also joy,—suffering which we would not be without (not for the human sympathy which it brings, for it brings us none, but) for the secret desire which we feel growing stronger within us every day, the desire of finding out God's will concerning us, and of doing it.

I have tried to describe as simply as I could the kind of way in which ordinary vocations generally come. If you recognize it as something like what you have known in your own experience, I think it may be safely concluded that God has given you, or is giving you, a special vocation. But is it a vocation to Evangelical Perfection? Let us see if we can find an answer to this question, for that is what we really want to know; and let us bear in mind that, since God calls all His children to some kind of perfection, *i.e.*, to the perfection of their state, when we speak throughout these pages of "perfection" as implying a special vocation, we wish to be understood as referring only to the perfection of the Counsels,— Evangelical Perfection.

If our reason is always reminding us of the greatness of God, and of our own littleness, of His exclusive rights over us, and of our absolute dependence on Him, so that we see the danger as well as the folly of living in the enjoyment of creatures, and come more and more to own the necessity of making God our All—this, probably, is a call to perfection.

If the world, though we know it to be dangerous, is also attractive, and we feel that the only chance of safety for us is to break with it altogether—this is still more probably a call to perfection. If we realize for ourselves practically, what we have always held in theory, that "the friendship of the world is enmity with God," and that, in trying to reconcile the two, we are (to use St. James's words) "adulterers and adulteresses;" if we know that for *us*, at least, the only hope of salvation is to be "violent," and take the kingdom of heaven by force, then undoubtedly this is a call to perfection.

Or if our soul is athirst for God, so that it

longs for Him as the hart for the waterbrooks; if everything that is not God sickens us, and our whole self is crying out to Him asking to be satisfied with Himself, and restless because it has not yet attained to Him; if this thirst and this desire increase with delay, if, in spite of everything seeming to be against us, we lose neither our hope nor our confidence; this again proves, I think, a call to perfection.

Or if we feel our heart drawn with a strange new drawing to share the lot of Jesus upon earth; if the beauty of the Passion makes us long to suffer; if the sight of the crucifix inflames us with the desire of union with the Crucified; if we find ourselves welcoming the sorrows of our daily life, and rejoicing in worldly failure, and growing indifferent to misfortunes, and thriving under temptation, then most certainly this is a call to perfection.

A mere wish to imitate the saints, or any one particular saint, is no proof of a call to perfection, but rather the contrary. Many souls, I think, fall into this delusion. They read the Lives of the Saints, and grow hot as they read; they imagine that by doing what the saints did, they themselves will be able to arrive at perfection. They do not see that it is not *what* the saints did, but *how* they did it, that made them what they were. The saints lived in the power of the Holy Spirit, and did all things as Jesus did them, to the glory of God the Father. That was the secret of their perfection, and it must be the secret of ours. So, truly shall we be followers of them as they are of Christ; but our own vocation comes not from any saint, but from the Saint of saints, Jesus, and He says, " Follow Me." Nothing less than this is a call to perfection.

A desire to be perfect within certain limits; a determination to go so far, but no farther ; a wish for greater holiness, coupled with human respect, or tempered with human prudence, proves that at present there is no call to perfection.

A desire to be perfect in order that we may receive the praise of men is a delusion quickly exploded, " All that will live godly in Christ Jesus must suffer persecution." Men may tolerate common holiness, but they will never praise perfection. Those who desire human applause had better seek it some other way. The servant is not greater than his Lord ; men said of our Master that

He had a devil, and was mad. And in proportion as we grow like Him they will say the same of us.

Are we in doubt about our own vocation, sisters? Perfection means being made altogether like Jesus; drinking of the cup that He drank of, and being baptized with the baptism that He was baptized withal. Are we able? When we look into our own souls, and see what His grace has done for us already, surely we need not fear to say, in full reliance upon Him, "We are able."

We shall indeed drink of His cup, and we shall drink of it very soon. Our vocation to perfection may no longer be a matter of doubt to us, but as soon as we recognize it and begin to respond to it, it will become a matter of perplexity to others. They will find us suddenly (so it seems to them), taking a new and an unusual view of things. What we formerly liked we have now ceased to care for. We are not so lively as we used to be, we do not so often say clever things, we are altogether more tame and uninteresting. At first they think it is a fancy which will wear off, an experiment which we shall grow tired of, but when they find that it is neither one nor the other they begin to feel annoyed.

They sometimes say things which hurt us, and, what is much worse, we know that we often do things which wound them. They are really so much better than we, that it seems presumptuous to think that we should be aiming higher than they, till we remember that it is God Who has chosen us, not we who have chosen Him. Still, this collision of feeling between ourselves and our dearest friends is a most terrible pain, and is only to be endured in union with Him Whose brethren did not believe in Him, and Who became a stranger unto them. To souls who are naturally loving, and whose family affection is strong, this is perhaps the greatest trial that the call to perfection brings. We have to be continually reminding ourselves that our life is to be guided no longer by natural, but by supernatural principles ; and even then the sorrow of wounding our friends is so intense that nothing but most special grace can carry us through it. We see what they do not, and are bound to the observance of precepts to which they are not called ; no wonder that we suffer, and they too. But we realize for our comfort what they cannot realize, that Jesus came " Not to send peace on earth, but a sword ; for He came to set a man at variance against his father, and the daughter against her mother;" and a man's foes, He has said, " shall be they of his own household." If this is what Christ came to do, let us rejoice that it is being done. It is our friends, not we, who are most to be pitied here.

A further possible trial may be that the priest under whose direction we are, will not, or cannot, recognize our vocation. This is indeed a most grievous trial, but it should not too much dishearten us. I take it for granted that we are living more or less under direction, and later on I will try to say something more about this ; only I must mention in this place that if we have been going on without direction hitherto, we ought not to delay to seek it now. Souls aspiring to perfection will almost certainly come to grief if they attempt to direct themselves.

A hard director who does not understand us, who checks our zeal, and suspects our enthusiasm, who freezes us by his coldness, and makes us suffer in every possible way, is far better than none, is perhaps the very director whom we really need. In whatever light he may view our vocation, if only we are faithful, he cannot hinder it. If he tries to check it, let us be patient; if it be divine it will survive his treatment, and if it does not survive his treatment the failure will only prove his sagacity.

Let us be persuaded, sisters, that vocation is so noble a thing that nothing can frustrate it except our own infidelity to its grace. It may be checked for years, and grow all the stronger for being checked; it can never be lost except through our own fault. A vocation guarded in spite of discouragements is especially dear to God. Only let us trust Him, and since it is His own glory that He has in view, let us be sure that when the right time for it comes our vocation will be acknowledged, and we shall know that the joy that such an acknowledgment brings is worth long years of waiting. Meanwhile let us be faithful and docile.

Let us never, therefore, through our own fault omit anything which we know to be a duty. We must be regular in our prayers, and, above all, we must attend the sacraments frequently and devoutly. You will, perhaps, think that I exaggerate when I say that our whole future may depend upon a single sacrament; but I believe it to be true. During this period, a confession shirked, a communion delayed, *may* cost us our vocation. I do not say that it will, but I feel sure that it may. This is a time when everyone but God seems against us; surely, then, we cannot afford to dispense with any opportunity of grace.

Further, let us be docile. We must not have preconceived ideas of what God means us to do. We must not try to hasten His grace, except by prayer, and even this should be very humbly done. Still less must we try to persuade our director into our own views about ourselves. It would be very well if we could cease from having any such views, for it would be the safest and most likely means of becoming docile. It is enough for us at present to know that God has called us to perfection; but we have yet to learn what that means, and it can only be learnt through suffering and prayer. Let us hold fast by God, and do nothing without Him; He will shew us how great things we must suffer for His sake. May He be praised above all for ever!

LETTER III.

Of the Religious and the Secular States.

A QUESTION which will certainly come into our minds in connection with our vocation, my sisters, is that of the religious life. In trying to respond to the call to perfection, which we can no longer doubt is ours, we find ourselves out of harmony with the world around us; and this not only at first, but increasingly, every day. To use a common expression, we feel so completely out of our element, that it seems quite impossible that God should intend us to remain where we are—*i.e.*, in the state technically called "secular." The thought presses upon us, whether we like it or not, that it would be better if we were to withdraw from the world altogether. The idea of the religious life naturally comes before us, and it is right that it should. For to many souls the call to perfection means also a call to the religious state; to so many, indeed, that the two things, though not in themselves the same, have come to be generally considered identical.

It is true that a vocation to religion

always means a call to perfection, but it is not true that the call to perfection means in all cases a call to religion. It is a question, however, which everyone who aims at perfection (remember that in these letters, by this is always meant *Evangelical* Perfection) must face sooner or later : " Does God Who has called me to follow Him in this way intend me also for the religious state ? or does He mean me to observe His Counsels here, in the midst of the world ? "

In considering this matter we must try to understand what is meant by " religion." Religion means "binding ;" a religious is one who is " bound." Those whom God calls into holy religion bind themselves by vows to observe the Counsels of Perfection; so that what may be a matter of devotion to others becomes an obligation to them. They voluntarily renounce the liberty which God has given them, and offer Him the most glorious of all sacrifices—that of their freedom. Like Jesus, Who was rich, they make themselves poor. They strip themselves, not only of their worldly possessions, but also of their earthly affections, their desires, and their will. They die to everything natural, that they may live altogether supernaturally. They are dead, and their life is hid with Christ in God. Their treasure is in heaven, their heart is also there; nothing remains of them on earth but their mortified members, the bodies which they daily offer in sacrifice to God.

Do not misunderstand me, my sisters; I speak of a death which is a real sacrifice to the persons thus making it; there is no virtue where there is no sacrifice. A heart that is naturally cold, that only loves with an effort, and that does not know what strong affections are, is about as different from a loving heart that has become supernaturally detached, as two things can possibly be. The first kind of detachment is a defect of nature, the latter is a triumph of grace. If it be true, which no doubt it is, that perfection thrives in the rarified atmosphere of spiritual detachment and solitude, it is rather because of its own internal heat, which enables it to live where otherwise life would be impossible. A cold heart is a self-centred heart, but true detachment finds its centre in God, and from that centre it draws a circle which embraces in its affections all things that God has made. Solitude contracts the self-centred soul, while it expands the soul which is divinely centred.

But religion means, technically, something more than this. The observance under vows of the Evangelical Counsels is not at all impossible in the secular state. A religious, in the stricter sense of the word, also lives in subjection to the rule of her society; she is one of a community, and her own individuality is not recognized, except in so far as it may profit to the common good. This does not mean that the life of a religious ought to be in any way mechanical; on the contrary, it should be a reasonable service in the highest sense of the word, her powers, whether of body or mind, being used for the general good of all, that the spirit of the community may be preserved in spite of, perhaps, apparent loss to the individual. A well-ordered community is like the Catholic Church in miniature; its members are all made to drink into one spirit. "They are many members, yet but one body;" those members of the body which seem to be feeble are necessary, and the whole is tempered together that there should be no division in the body, but that the members should have the same care one for another; and "whether one member suffer all the members suffer with it, or one member be honoured all the members rejoice with it" (1 *Cor.* xii. 20, 26). All this is implied in the very word "community," which means a society of people having common rights and interests. How the thought of it takes us back to those apostolic days of which we read: "The multitude of them that believed were of one heart and one soul: neither said any of them that aught of the things that he possessed was his own; but they had all things common" (*Acts* iv. 32).

Religious societies may be either cloistered or uncloistered, and the life may be active, contemplative, or mixed; that is to say, partly active and partly contemplative. In the beginnings of monasticism, religious orders were almost entirely contemplative, and active religious societies as now existing were unknown until the seventeenth century.* We must not suppose that contemplative religious do nothing but pray; manual work forms an essential part of their rule; and in the early ages, and indeed for many centuries, the Church and the world were alike

* The reader is referred to a pamphlet entitled "Uncloistered Sisterhoods."—London: Bale.

indebted to them for their intellectual labours. The "higher education of women," a phrase familiar to us to-day as associated with so much that is unwomanly, as well as unchristian, was a very practical part of the conventual system of mediæval times; times which it is fashionable to despise as dark and ignorant, but many of whose learned women were no whit inferior to the female student of the present day.

Later on, when the invention of printing and machinery accelerated the speed of life, active societies were required in order to keep pace with the times. The pamphlet already referred to gives so interesting a sketch of their development that I need not enter more into this subject, and those whom it interests cannot do better than read this little book. These active religious, or sisters of charity as they came to be called, have been probably kept in existence by the invisible support of the contemplatives, part of whose work it is to assist by their prayers those who are thus labouring for God in more external ways. Active religious generally get a certain amount of credit from the world, on account of their visible labours in schools, missions, hospitals,

&c.; while in these days contemplatives are invariably the object of unmitigated suspicion and contempt to those who can only appreciate what appears on the surface. The revival of sisterhoods among ourselves is mostly an attempt to combine the two lives, but with a strong tendency to activity rather than to contemplation. In these days a purely contemplative vocation is comparatively rare, and in England contemplative religious societies can hardly be said to exist. They are contrary to the spirit of the age. I think, my sisters, that, considering what the spirit of the age is, the fact that anything is contrary to it is an argument very highly in its favour. An "Our Father" said every day for the restoration among us of contemplative religion would be an act of true patriotic charity.

Everything in the religious life is done according to rule, and order is observed in all. There is a time to work and a time to pray, and a time in which to take recreation: one thing is not allowed to interfere with another, and so a general harmony is preserved. The same order and the same rule go on day by day, month by month, and year by year, with a monotony which (in the case of the more cloistered communities) is rarely, if ever, broken. To some of us this monotony looks very attractive; it suggests thoughts of the operations of God within Himself, and of His order in the world of nature,—the laws which shall not be broken. There is a rest about it which contrasts greatly with the wearying variety of the world. We feel that it would be good to be here. Others, again, are afraid that their perseverance would not be equal to the continuous strain, yet they would admit that, though the religious state may be hard to live in, it is the state of all others in which they would like to die.

The *aim* of the religious is precisely the same as that of the secular who aims at perfection—viz., detachment from creatures and union with God; but her *state* is very different. The religious has the support of her community. She is one of a body, and must carefully avoid anything like singularity. Whatever her own individual character may be, she is bound to sink that, so far as it may estrange her from her sisters, and she must act in all respects exactly according to the spirit of her society, doing what those around her do.

Hence the importance as to choice of community. Some good persons with mistaken views of God imagine that the call to religion means not only the mortification of their evil nature, but the annihilation of their individuality. Self has to be crucified, that Christ may live in us; then truly will be restored in us the divine likeness that we have lost. But if we annihilate self there can be no possibility of likeness to God, for we are made to reflect Him in ourselves. Thus: a mirror may be made to reflect the sun—if dulled, it must be brightened in order that the reflection may be perfect; but if you remove the mercury the power of reflecting is gone. Man is a mirror to reflect God, and his individuality is like the mercury, which makes reflection possible. In choosing a community therefore, it is right to follow, rather than to resist, any reasonable attraction which may be felt to one rather than another. A person much disposed to prayer would be mistaken in seeking to mortify this taste by joining a society chiefly occupied in external works of mercy.

Our Lord needs His Maries in these days no less than formerly, and they are not at all bound to resist the call to contemplation, merely because they find pleasure in following it. How comes it that, after all our experience of God's loving kindness, we are so suspicious both of Him and of His gifts? If He has given us a particular attraction it is because, in following it, we shall find our best way to pleasing Him, and not for the mere purpose of having to resist it in order to secure our salvation. Surely it should be beneath us to have such unloving thoughts of God as this implies.

It may be as well to notice, in connection with the choice of community, that it not unfrequently happens that a person with a real religious vocation seeks admission into a society for which she is quite unfitted. This will be very likely to happen where an attraction has been resisted. Abroad, on the continent, a postulant rejected by the religious of one order, or herself withdrawing from them, passes on to another, and it may be to several, until at last she finds the one for which God intends her. But we, in England, with our insular way of viewing everything, will scarcely admit the religious vocation of any person who fails to accommodate herself to the first sisterhood that comes in her way, no matter how much opposed to her own genius the spirit of it may be. We expect squares to fit into circles just as easily as they would into squares, and we are annoyed with them for not doing so. The fancy which I am afraid some people indulge in of going from one community to another, out of mere curiosity, cannot be too strongly condemned; but, on the other hand, we may venture to hope that somewhat more elasticity in the choice of community may, as time goes on, be accorded to religious aspirants.

Having tried to get some idea as to what is meant by the religious state, let us now consider the state technically known as "secular." Secular means having to do with the age—*i.e.*, with the present world; and the secular, as distinguished from the religious, is one who does not live in community, but in the midst of ordinary society. Those who are called to perfection in the world, and who observe the counsels under vows, are, to a certain degree, "religious," though not in the perfect state of religion; and to such the "world" may be said to mean all persons who are leading an ordinary christian life, as distinguished from the life of the counsels, as well as those who are mere worldlings—that is, who are living for this world only.

Now, just as the religious is prone to regard with contempt those who are technically called "seculars," and to class them as mere worldlings, so the secular, who aims at perfection, is liable to a similar fault. Let us have courage, dear sisters, at the outset to face this ugly fact. Pride is the besetting temptation of those who aspire to perfection. This does not look well in print; but since it is true, it concerns us to know it, for in proportion as we desire to be perfect we shall be tempted to pride. There are, no doubt, many reasons for this, but the fact itself is so patent that we need not trouble ourselves just now with the reasons. The question is, How are we to meet it?

First of all, then, we must have a clear notion of what is meant by "the world," and of our own position in it as Christians bound to observe the counsels, and to live a separated, though uncloistered, life.

If by "the world" we mean that kingdom of which the devil is the prince, and whose friendship is enmity with God, it is evident that we can make no truce with it whatever. We must meet it sword in hand, and resist it unto blood, striving against sin. But if we mean by "the world" the society of our christian friends and acquaintance—our fellow-communicants—then, in the common course of events, we need not look to be either in open or in secret hostility with it. It may be quite true that, having received a higher call than others, we are bound to aim at a higher perfection, and to lead a stricter life as a means towards that end. But we are not on that account to despise them as a race of beings inferior to ourselves. They may be serving God according to their lights far better than we are serving Him according to ours. If their grace is less, so also most probably are their sins; and if they are doing to the utmost of their power all that they know to be right, and carefully avoiding all that they know to be wrong, that is more, perhaps, than can be truthfully said of us. Let us be very careful never to judge others because, as we think, their standard is not so high as our own. If it is the standard which God intends for them, in aiming at it they will arrive at the degree of perfection to which He has called them; and in finding fault with them for not having the same standard as ourselves we shall not only be doing them no good, but shall be doing ourselves very serious harm. After all, vocation is a grace, and if we have received a higher call than some others, that is a matter for humility, and certainly not for pride. The greater our grace, the greater our possible fall. They who are called to walk in high places, are safe only so far as they are humble.

But the secular who aims at perfection needs courage no less than humility. Unlike the religious, she has no visible support of any kind. In the world, yet not of the world, she is bound more or less to be singular, which does not at all mean that she is to be eccentric, but simply that she must be content to be isolated, the word "singular" meaning to exist by itself. The position of the religious is recognized, and for the most part honoured; but the secular who aims at perfection is the object more or less of ridicule, and is denied a right to any position at all. I speak of what is generally the case, though I doubt not there are happy exceptions. For the most part, religious do not encourage the idea of perfection in the world; some will even deny it to be possible; while as for seculars who have not themselves received this call, what can they be expected to know about it? The most that we can look for from them is, that they will charitably allow us to go on our own way without forcing us to unnecessary conflict. More will be said about this later on, so we need not enlarge upon it here ; but if the lowest degree of abjection (abjection means that which is only fit to be thrown away as refuse,) is that most to be desired in the spiritual life, I imagine that some truly heroic souls would choose to serve God perfectly in the secular state, that is, if they had any power of choice left, for outwardly it is a state of very great abjection ; well if the interior abjection be as great !

The life of perfection, whether religious or secular, is one of very special temptation. All the powers of evil will league themselves together to vex and torment the soul which thus tries to yield itself altogether to God. Temptations of the thoughts, the desires, and the affections will assail it in turn or all at once. Doubts as to its vocation, as to the use of the Sacraments, the grace of God, the very faith itself, and other nameless trials, will not cease to torment it ; and what will the soul in this condition do ? It will recognize more and more its call to perfection, and will endure as seeing Him Who is invisible, rejoicing that it is counted worthy to suffer for His sake.

But in which of these states are we to serve God? This, let us remember, is a question of vocation, for if we would be perfect we can neither safely remain in the secular state, nor wisely enter the state of religion without a distinct, divine call. Some souls will arrive at perfection in the world, who would not even be passably good in religion, and many will arrive at perfection in religion, who would never be able to persevere in the world. It is a matter to be referred to our director, and by him possibly to some others, who will consider with him the circumstances of our life, and our individual temperament or character, before arriving at any decision. Two things, however, should be specially noted here. First, that no desire for the religious state, however earnest, is any proof of our being called to it, just as no shrinking from the religious state is any proof that we are not called to it. God's desire for us, not our desire for ourselves, constitutes vocation. Secondly, that no decision given by our superiors, either in favour of, or against our having a vocation is infallibly conclusive. We may bid fair at first to make most excellent religious, and yet break down in the very early days of our noviciate; while, on the other hand, our vocation may be denied at first, only to ripen secretly, and to be acknowledged later on. What has been already said about vocation to perfection holds good here also; so long as *we* are faithful it cannot be lost. Vocations are divine things, with a supernatural vitality of their own, and a power, not only of living but of thriving in any atmosphere, and under any conditions that are not in themselves sinful. Opposition, rightly met, only ensures more vigorous and certain growth.

Every delay in the spiritual life has its own particular work to do in the soul. This is especially true of delays affecting vocation. It is a truth, however, which we are very slow to learn; some of us never learn it at all till it is too late. The call to religion comes to us in early childhood perhaps, and follows us through much that would check it altogether if it were not divine. In our good moments we wish to respond to it, and it is always hidden in our heart among our best treasures. But time goes on, and we are not free to follow it yet. At present, and for years to come, our duty is, and probably will be, in the world. Now is the time to watch and pray, and be patient. Woe unto us if we lose patience! for how do we know that it will not mean losing our vocation too? Yet this is the case with many. Because they cannot immediately have what they desire, they imagine that they may safely amuse themselves with the world. Because some people can do certain things innocently enough, they think that they can do the same. They forget that others may have received no call to live differently, but that *they* have. God has set His choice upon them; He wants them peculiarly for Himself. It is disloyalty to Him, as well as folly to their own interests, to grow impatient of delay. Happily His long-suffering is greater than theirs, yet, in spite of it, how many souls lose their religious vocation by their misuse of this precious time. It is meant for probation, for self-discipline, and for laying those solid foundations upon which alone heroic sanctity can be built. There is only one safe course for that soul to pursue, which, having a call to religion, is at present hindered from following it ; and that is, patiently and prayerfully, without ostentation, but very bravely, to observe the Counsels of Perfection, and to live as far as circumstances will permit, like a religious in the midst of the world.

And those of us, my sisters, who really are not called to the religious state, what are we to do ? Are we to give up aiming at perfection ? is there no alternative but to go into a convent or else to belong to that multitude of Christians who make the best of this world, and yet hope to have an equal reward hereafter with those who here have forsaken all for Christ ? Is perfection in the secular state, though possible in theory, impossible in practice, so that we must really go back and be as we were before ? There are many who will tell us so, but we will not, we need not, believe them. Thanks be to God it is *He*, not man, Who has given us our vocation ; and when Jesus says to any soul, " Follow thou Me," who shall dare to forbid ?

I should like to ask such persons as persist in confounding the life of perfection with the monastic life, what they think was our

Lord's meaning when He gave the Evangelical Counsels to that young man? Did He mean that he was to become what is technically called a monk? Did He not know that religious communities, as we understand them, would not exist for some centuries later? Excepting for the blessed martyrs, was there to be no possibility of Evangelical Perfection until in the fourth century the fathers of the desert established the monastic life? Since our Lord Jesus Christ is the same yesterday, to-day, and for ever, His Counsels are unchanging as Himself, and are true for all time; and are always to be received by those to whom it is given to receive them.

Moreover, the call to the religious or monastic state, supposes certain qualifications which cannot be thought essential to perfection. Vocation to perfection is independent of a person's state of health, of domestic circumstances, individual temperament, and so on, all of which should be taken serious account of before anyone enters a community. This latter call is purely interior, and cannot therefore be thought to depend upon a capacity for living on vegetables and practising bodily austerities, which would often be part of a religious rule. A high spiritual aim is probably the best of all cures for physical indispositions, yet it must be owned that certain exterior conditions make the religious state an impossibility for some. But if this is taken to prove that such persons have no call to perfection, that is making perfection to depend not on the interior dispositions of the soul only, but also on many outward circumstances entirely independent of the person's goodwill; not simply in purifying the heart and mortifying the spirit and senses, but also in wearing a habit, eating certain kinds of food, and living in community. Such a doctrine is nowhere to be found in the Gospel of Jesus Christ.

In order to meet this difficulty we sometimes hear it said that such an one has an "interior call" to the religious state, but not an "exterior call," which is all the same as saying that God is sometimes in contradiction with Himself, and calls two ways at once. Do not let us dishonour Him either by inventing or by believing any such vagaries. He never gives a vocation without enabling us sooner or later to follow it. He loves His creatures far too well to torture them thus. Vocation is the expression of His will for the soul, and that which He wills us to do He enables us to do.

We may desire the religious state for ourselves; but of what good is that, unless God desires it for us? It is quite possible to wish wrongly a right thing. Desires for religion are not by any means necessarily religious desires. We must submit any such wishes to a very honest scrutiny, or we may become, without knowing it, the unhappy victims of spiritual ambition, pride, and discontent. Let us take as an axiom of the spiritual life that nothing is religious that is not disciplined; it will save us from many an illusion.

On the other hand, let us beware lest, through a false discretion, we fail to respond to our call. If God points out to us the way of Evangelical Perfection as that wherein He desires that we should walk, there can be no alternative for us. Perfection may be learnt in the world, in spite of all that the world (and, alas! too many religious), may say to the contrary. And if this be God's choice for us, then, of course, it is our vocation; and at all risks, and in spite of all difficulties we will rise up and follow it. "No man, having put his hand to the plough, and looking back, is fit for the kingdom of God" (*St. Luke* ix. 62).

We have put our hand to the plough; and now that we find the work to be not quite what we thought it was, and that "perfection" for us does not mean what is technically called "religion," are we looking back? Surely not! Our vocation may mean something very different from what we hoped at first, yet we would not miss it for the world. To know that God has a special purpose concerning us, that He has chosen us for Himself, to perfect us through suffering, for a union with Himself of the deepest intimacy, is enough to make us wonderfully happy. Without leaving our present sphere of life, we are to follow Jesus in His Counsels of Perfection, and while seeming to be as one of those in the midst of whom we live, we are to aspire to heights unknown to them, and which it would be rash indeed for us to attempt to scale, were it not for that secret vocation which it would be a worse folly to despise. So, then, let us remain in the world, and if duty demands it let us remain in our own home; and there, in the midst of all that goes to make the pleasure and the happiness of those around us, let us grow into the deeper meaning of these words of Christ: "If any man come to Me, and hate not his father, and mother, and wife, and children, and brethren, and sisters, yea, and his own life also, he cannot be My disciple" (*St. Luke* xiv. 26).

If any souls need to be sure that they have a divine vocation, it is those whom God calls to be perfect in the secular state, for the temptations of this life are such as can only be safely met on firm ground. Simplicity of intention and complete docility to their director are essential, or they will soon find themselves in a very quagmire of spiritual selfishness, and will be a cross to their neighbours as well as a burden to themselves. But for souls who know the will of God concerning them, there is nothing to fear, for if the discipline of their training is terrible, grace to bear it will be given, and the more they have to suffer the more they will learn to love.

Has God given us this vocation, my sisters? Are we called to the life of Evangelical Perfection in the world? Then we are left altogether to Him. Henceforth let no man trouble us: we are God's foundlings; His special charge. Let us abandon ourselves entirely to His most dear and blessed Will, that He may be glorified in us, and we in Him. To Him be praise for ever!

LETTER IV.
Of Evangelical Poverty.

JESUS be with you, sisters, and may His poverty be riches unto us!

We have already seen that the aim of the religious and of the secular who has received the call to perfection is the same—viz., detachment from creatures and union with God. Their interior principle is one, it is only their exterior state that differs. This principle is fulfilled and this aim is reached, by the faithful observance of the Counsels which our Lord in the Gospel enjoins upon those who would be perfect. Souls whom God calls to perfection, yet keeps in the world, must remember that the observance of the Counsels is as necessary for them as for religious. It is impossible to be perfect any other way.

This being so, it is important to understand, first, what the Evangelical Counsels are, and then the manner in which they may be observed by persons living in the world. We shall see that it means entering altogether upon another kind of life, for though our outward circumstances may continue just what they were, the spirit in which we meet them must be different.

In thinking of the Evangelical Counsels, and still more in speaking or writing of them, we find ourselves in a certain difficulty. It is hard to separate one from the other, because they can none of them be said to have any independent existence. In trying to practise them we soon discover that one Counsel involves another, and that all are implied in each. Just as in the Most Holy Trinity each Person, though distinct, does not exist by Himself, but lives and acts in and by the Others; so it is with the Counsels —These three are one. But as the Eternal Father is the Fount of Being in the Godhead, so I think it is true to say that holy poverty is the source of Evangelical Perfection. In sharing the poverty of Jesus we become chaste in body and in soul, and we are made partakers also of His obedience.

We must never forget that in aiming at

perfection it is Jesus Who is at once our Teacher and our Model. We do not set ourselves to imitate this or that particular saint, but we come to drink into the spirit of Jesus, to share His mind, and to partake of His Nature. The Gospel becomes our text-book, the Cross our standard, the Crucified our Master. We go to Him to be taught, and we find that as soon as He opens His mouth to teach it is to speak of poverty— "Blessed are the poor in spirit, for theirs is the kingdom of heaven"; just as later on we hear Him saying, "Sell all that thou hast, and give to the poor, and thou shalt have treasure in Heaven." The poverty which Christ enjoins is that which He practised Himself, it is to be "voluntary" and "actual."

A thing is voluntary when it is our own free choice for ourselves. The poverty of Jesus was voluntary. He was rich, yet for our sakes He became poor. The poverty of St. Peter and the other Apostles was voluntary —they forsook all that they had and followed Him. The poverty of an envious beggar is not voluntary, for if he could he would be rich.

A thing is actual that exists truly and

absolutely. The poverty of Jesus was actual. He was born in a stable and laid in a manger, because there was no room for Him anywhere else. He died upon a Cross, and was buried by the charity of friends. The poverty of the Apostles was also actual. St. Peter could truly say, " Silver and gold have I none," and St. Paul worked as a tent-maker for his living. The poverty of an envious beggar may also be actual, but there is nothing about it either christian or apostolic. From which we see that "actual" poverty must also be "voluntary" before it can be said to be "evangelical:" that which sanctifies poverty and makes it holy is the willingness with which it is undertaken or accepted.

This is the kind of poverty which Christ declares to be blessed, and which He counsels. Evangelical poverty consists in detaching ourselves from everything we possess. There are no doubt different degrees of evangelical poverty, and all persons are not called to the highest, which is total absence of any earthly goods whatever; but everyone who is called to perfection is bound, at least, to that poverty of spirit which consists in a willingness and a desire to be poor and to suffer loss for Christ's sake. In heart and spirit the perfect Christian will always regard himself as having nothing.

This, I think, exactly describes the state of mind at which we ought to aim, or, rather, it gives us the key-note of the rule in following which we can most safely and unobtrusively advance towards perfection, while still remaining in the world. In some respects poverty may be more easily practised in the cloister than in the secular state. On entering religion the whole of a person's worldly goods is yielded up for the benefit of the community: and the poverty of this state consists rather in having no personal possessions than in the endurance of absolute want. Comparatively few religious orders depend for their sustenance either upon charity or their own manual labour; and it cannot be denied that some persons who enter religion are practically better off than they would be in the world. Religious poverty therefore is not, strictly speaking, "actual." No individual of the community can say that "aught that she possesses is her own," but it cannot be said of the community, as a whole, that it actually possesses nothing, although the spirit of poverty may reign in all its members in a very eminent degree.

Now, just as the religious actually resigns all personal claim to her own possessions for the good of the community, so quite as really, though less apparently, the secular who is preparing for the religious state, or whose vocation it is to be perfect in the world, will in spirit and intention absolutely resign all right to everything that may be hers.

She may not be called upon to suffer serious want, or to go without necessaries, but then neither, for the most part, are religious. Like these, however, she may be most truly "poor in spirit," and not only feel, but *realize*, in the practical experience of every-day life that "nothing of aught she possesses is her own."

If, dear sisters, I might mention (without fear of seeming childish) what I believe to be the simplest way of cultivating in our-ourselves this spirit of holy poverty, I should advise that the possessive pronouns "my" and "mine" be allowed to drop out of our vocabulary. Of course there are occasions when, to avoid pedantry, they must be used; but let it be always with a mental protest to ourselves. In following this very simple, and quite unnoticeable, rule, it is wonderful how soon we come to realize that we indeed "possess nothing." No one has any rights except to those things he can call his own; and if we make a point of never calling anything our own, we at once deprive ourselves of all our rights. In some religious communities the plural possessive " our " is used .instead of the singular "my." This would, of course, be meaningless in the world; but no one knows, who has not tried it, how easy it generally is to avoid saying of a thing, "it is *mine*," or, "it belongs to *me*." If other people take a fancy, whether to our ornaments, books, clothes, or what not, and like to appropriate them, we can very well let them go, when we remember that our only real possession now is God, and our only rights His. What is the cause of more than half the lawsuits in the world, and of nearly all the quarrels, but this—the contending for rights? Yet the Master Whom we serve has said, "If any man will sue thee at the law, and take away thy coat, forbid him not to have thy cloak also." And St. Paul tells us that, rather than stand up for our rights, we are to suffer ourselves to be defrauded.

Let us try to act consistently upon this principle, and we shall feel ourselves before long entering into the spirit of Christ, in a way which we should never have thought possible. If we draw up for ourselves some practical rule having this for its basis, and carry it into all the details of daily life, it will work an incredible change in our general view of things. We shall see how very worthless everything is but God. We shall find ourselves more at leisure, for it takes time to make others recognize our rights, however apparent they may be to us; and here also we shall reap the fruit of peace, for unlike much else that is involved in the practice of perfection, *this* will give no annoyance to our neighbours, who will unconsciously gain at our expense, and be quite satisfied. By degrees, also, let us part with everything for which we have a particular affection, and those treasures which others have been kind enough still to leave in our possession let us willingly make presents of to them. It is a good way of learning detachment, and a simple one.

If God calls us to something more than this, so that at His bidding we may literally strip ourselves of all worldly possessions for

Christ's sake and the Gospel's, happy are we! But it often pleases Him that we should act as His almoners, and, while seeming to possess this world's goods, be really His stewards, using them not for our own comfort, but for His glory and the good of our brethren. We must bear in mind that wealth, like other talents, is a gift, and it is no more sinful for one to be rich than for another to be handsome, or another musical. Everything we have is God's, not ours, and they who would be perfect must give all back to Him, and keep nothing for themselves. Let those who have money make a rule of spending none on their own mere comfort or pleasure, *and let their ideas of what is necessary be as limited as possible.* If, in order to please others, they have sometimes to spend money, as it seems to them, needlessly, it may be done with a holy interior motive, and the seeming extravagance will bring its own reward by concealing their real aim. No one, *e.g.*, who out of deference to the wishes of others, and in order to hide grace, spends on house decorating what he would much rather give in charity, will ever be suspected of aiming at Evangelical Perfection. Yet the person who cheerfully acted thus would be most truly poor in spirit, and most entirely obedient. Discretion, charity, and a modest light-heartedness, will best teach us in what ways we, who are in the world, can practise holy poverty without attracting to ourselves either praise or blame.

Some of us, perhaps, are actually poor—it is the portion God has chosen for us; can we, then, hope for that voluntary poverty which alone is Evangelical? If we are content with our lot, and do not wish to improve upon it, undoubtedly we can. If we go beyond this, and love our poverty because it is the portion God chose for Himself when on earth; if we feel that it is too good for us, both as being in itself more than we deserve, and also because it brings us such wonderful possibilities of union with Him; we are not far off the very highest degree of Evangelical poverty.

But this Counsel of perfection does not merely apply to such visible possessions as houses, money, and lands. It has a far wider and deeper and more spiritual significance, which we will consider by itself in another letter.

Meanwhile, my sisters, let us honestly see

how we can reduce to practice the points we have been thinking of. "We brought nothing into the world, and it is certain we can carry nothing out." This is true of every one. But we who are called to perfection have a steep ascent to climb, and if we hope to reach the top we must be content to go barefoot, and, save for the cross that we carry, empty-handed too. Only they who forsake *all* can follow Jesus to perfection.

We read in the Acts of the Apostles that "a certain man and his wife sold a possession, and kept back part of the price, and brought a certain part, and laid it at the Apostles' feet," pretending it was the whole. We know their end. But, my sisters, where is the difference between their sin and that of souls who, being called to perfection, and responding to the call, dare to have reserves with God? May He save us from such deceitfulness of riches, and give us grace to become altogether poor for His sake. To Him be praise for ever!

LETTER V.

Of Evangelical Poverty. (2.)

WE come now, dear sisters, to consider the Counsel of Evangelical Poverty, under its deeper and more spiritual aspect, namely, that of entire detachment, not only from temporal possessions, such as houses, money, and lands, but from all earthly things whatsoever. To limit this Counsel of holy poverty to the surrender of these merely external goods would be to limit the practice of perfection, and to make it possible only for those who are what the world calls rich. These external goods, moreover, are not really the best even of our temporal possessions, for there are many things which most of us hold far dearer. Such are, for example, health, talents, home, friendship, success, and reputation or character; from each and all of which we who aspire to perfection must become more and more detached.

Detachment might well be called the soul of Evangelical poverty; for unless in becoming poor we become also detached, our poverty will in no way help us to be perfect.

To detach means literally to "separate from," and that is precisely what we are called to do. We have to detach (separate) ourselves from everything created, in order that we may attach (bind) ourselves, solely and altogether, to God. Detachment is the means by which we arrive at perfection, and perfection is simply this,—attachment to, union with, God. The means, no doubt, is full of pain; but considering what the end is, this need cause us neither surprise nor regret. That creatures, such as we know ourselves to be, should be allowed, as the result of any process whatever, to arrive at perfection, is so wonderful a glory, that it is well worth any amount of suffering. Courage, my sisters! and with a good heart let us set ourselves at once to this work of detachment.

Our Lord has told us that, to whom much is given, of him much will be required. In other words, the more anyone happens to possess, from so much the more has he to become detached. We do not all possess many talents, but we all have one; and this one, by which I mean our life, embraces in itself whatever else we may happen to have. We then, who are called to perfection, have to lose our life for Christ's sake; it must be given up to Him that He may do with it according to His good pleasure.

Whatever may be included in this one talent, whether it be health, work, friendship, physical, mental, or spiritual capacity of any kind, belongs, let us remember, not to us, but to God. We are to use it not for our glory, but for His; and in order to do so we must detach ourselves from it, so that we really cease to care for it or have any interest in it whatever, except in so far as it helps us to do His will, and advance His kingdom.

Take, for instance, health. It is a favourite idol in this most idolatrous age. Like every other gift of the good God, people make it an end instead of a means; they fall down and worship it, and live for it, and waste time, and care, and thought, and words, and money upon it, and fret because it does not repay them for their devotion. And yet, what is the good of mere physical health except as a means whereby we may serve and toil for God? In itself, and viewed apart from its object, there are few gifts which so easily lead us away from Him. Great physical strength needs much grace to sanctify it, or it becomes a positive hindrance to our spiritual development. It is an axiom of the saints that, within certain limits, we must cease to have regard for our health. This does not mean that we are to take liberties with it which God never meant should be taken; but only that we are to be content with the degree of bodily health it pleases Him to give us, and not waste energy upon trying to improve it, or even to preserve it. Certainly it is the least to say, that if more souls aimed at perfection there would be fewer chronic invalids in the world. Let us detach ourselves, then, from anxiety as to our bodily health, for until we do this we shall never be able to take so much as one step towards Evangelical Perfection.

Next as to our work. From this, too, we must become detached. While working always with all our might, we must remember that it is God and not ourselves for Whom we work. We must be ready therefore at all times to leave, at His call, our present work for some other; we must not allow it to engross us, or to become in any way an end to us. We must learn to be quite indifferent as to the kind of work we do, and if we have our choice let us take that which is lowliest. Sometimes He will set us to tasks which we feel quite unequal to, and in which we know that we shall fail. If we are truly detached, it will matter little to us whether we fail or not. We shall remember that when God said of His work, "It is finished," He was hanging nailed to a Cross, in such apparent weakness that it was said of Him, "Himself He cannot save." So if our work brings us pain, or shame, or disappointment, it is only making us like Christ. We do our very best, and fail. Nobody cares for our work, nobody looks at it, nobody uses it; our time, our thought, our money perhaps, are all thrown away. No, dear sisters, a thousand times no! God's object in the work we had to do has been achieved; it is no failure in His sight, neither shall it be a failure in ours. It has helped to make us more detached, and every new lesson in detachment, believe me, is worth many failures.

We must be content, too, if need be, to leave our work incomplete. Man likes to turn out his work by the dozen or by the gross; God likes quality, not quantity, and we are working for Him; the patience, not the rapidity, with which a thing is done gives it beauty in His sight. Patience, let us remember, is in itself a perfect work. They who by detachment from creatures are becoming attached to God, can afford to be patient like Him. They, for whom eternity has already begun, have no need to hurry. Let us be diligent in our work, but let us also be patient; and if in the sight of men it always remains unfinished, God, Who judges rightly, will reckon our patience to us for perfection. We must leave the ending of all work in His hands Who is Himself our End, or we shall never become truly detached.

We must also learn detachment from places. Here we are strangers and pilgrims, having no abiding city. That which we call "home" to-day, another may call "home" to-morrow; reverse in fortune, our own death, or that of friends, may at any time call us away. Our only real home is in God. We live and move and have our being in Him; out of Him no rest is possible. Yet how slow we are to learn this. Of all the hard lessons which come to us in the way of detachment, I think this is one of the hardest. We get so fond of places; the house in which we live, the neighbourhood in which our duty lies, the church in which we worship, so often become a snare to us. They may all have come to us in the ordering of God's providence; they are not self-chosen, we are for the present just where He means us to be, and so far this is good, but we cannot bear to think of the changes that may be before us. It would be such a wrench to go away, the present home has become so dear to us, we cling to it so fondly, that life anywhere else, or under any other circumstances, is dreadful even to think of. All this is a hindrance to perfection; we shall never be perfect if we allow ourselves in such attachments. It would not be wise perhaps, even if it were possible, to change our circumstances, or by our own act to free ourselves from our surroundings, but we must courageously ask God to detach us from them. Such a prayer will infallibly be answered, not, perhaps, in the way or by the means which we anticipate, but in a manner of God's choosing the change will certainly come. His methods are gentler than we can imagine. Partings which we dreaded not long since, He orders so mercifully, that when the time comes we find the bitterness is past already. The home we used to love, the church we used to cling to, have ceased for some reason or other to be to us what they were. We think that they have altered; it may be that they have, but there has been a change in ourselves also. In unseen ways, so gentle that it may be we have been hardly conscious of them, God Himself has severed the ties which bound us to earth, and is binding us secretly to Himself instead.

From friends also we must become detached. That friendship only is secure which has its foundation in God. We can tolerate no other kind. However amiable, or useful, or attractive, people may be, they cannot be our friends unless we find that they really help us to love God more. Of course, in forming this rule we may sometimes chill or disappoint those who seek our friendship. Let us be affable to all, but familiar with very few; and let us be ready any day, at the call of God, to bid farewell even to these with a brave heart, and go on our way alone. Let us be assured, my sisters, that those love their friends most tenderly who love them in God and for God; and such love is not only the tenderest, but also the strongest; tender and strong in proportion as it is detached.

Next come our desires. Who that is human has no desires? They grow like grass in the spring-time, and help to keep us fresh, and save us many a while from idleness. Rightly directed, they are almost the most sanctifying influences of our natural life. Yet how easy it is to cling to our desires, and how fatal! Let us pray to be saved from inordinate desires, even for good things; our holiest wishes must be disciplined, our most ardent longings must be chastened, everything that we hope for either for ourselves or for others, in this world or the next, must be detached from us, and we from it, and so offered to God. Our very longings after perfection will become dangerous to us unless this is borne in mind.

A further degree of detachment consists in a willingness to be dishonoured for Christ's sake. There are few things that we value more than our good name. We like to be well thought of, at least by our friends. If strangers despise us we can forgive them, for we put it down to their ignorance, and think that they would appreciate us if they really knew us; but to be disdained by one's friends is hard to human nature. Yet we must make up our minds to hear no good of ourselves, if we are to become like Christ. They called Him a wine-bibber, a gluttonous man; they said that He was beside Himself, that He had a devil, that He was a blasphemer, a malefactor; indeed, there was no evil that men did not say of Him. And are we afraid of losing our good name? If so, where is our likeness to our Lord? where is our hope of perfection? We love human praise, yet profess to be the servants of a despised God; we are anxious to stand well with the world that crucified Him. Yet we have His own commandment about this very thing, and it bids us rejoice and be exceeding glad when men say all manner of evil against us falsely for His sake.

We may well fear that there is something wanting to us unless we are evil spoken of. They who take away our character, and who seek at all to injure our reputation, are really our best friends. They provide us with opportunities of growing like Jesus, which but for them we should never have. Let us welcome everything that helps to lower us in the sight of men; for woe unto us when they speak well of us! Only in proportion as we rejoice in the loss of our good name may we hope to share in the perfection of Jesus.

Lastly, we must learn detachment from spiritual consolations. Where is the merit of serving God gladly when all goes well with us, or even when, if others are against us, we feel that God is on our side? Spiritual consolations are the occasional refreshment, not the common food of the soul. Perfection is reached through long periods of dryness, desolation, and interior trials. First God allures the soul, then He brings her into the wilderness, and then He speaks comfortably to her. When first we enter on the perfect way, God allures us by His sweetness; but as time goes on we find ourselves in the wilderness, and there very often we shall find that we are to remain during the greater part of our life. Thus, in detaching us from spiritual delights, God attaches us the more securely to Himself. Let us never dishonour Him by asking for graces which, after all, might lead us to repose less entirely in Him. From time to time, when it pleases Him, He will speak comfortably to us. But let us remember always it is not His comforts, but *Himself* we want. This is the meaning of true detachment, and the end of evangelical poverty: that we possess nothing, either in this world or the next, but God only. To Him be praise for ever!

LETTER VI.

Of the Rewards of Evangelical Poverty.

WE must be on our guard, my sisters, against a very common fallacy which is likely to be a snare to uninstructed souls in aiming at perfection. We must never think that mere asceticism in itself is of any value whatever. It may seem an unnecessary caution to give in an age which, like the present, is so essentially the reverse of ascetic, but perhaps this is really the chief reason why so much caution is needed. The cross of Christ stands out in such bold contrast to the luxury of the world around us, that we who have received the call to Evangelical Perfection may be inclined perhaps to fall into an error which sets a value upon poverty for its own sake, and gives to shame a glory it was never meant to have. Let us remember always that there is no good whatever in the mere endurance of suffering, however noble or patient it be. The Passion of our Blessed Lord Jesus Christ was not an end, but a means. For the joy that was set before Him He endured the Cross. He suffered these things, and so, entered into glory. It must be the same with us; our light affliction, which is but for a moment, worketh for us an exceeding weight of glory; and it is not in the affliction, but in the glory, that our blessedness consists.

Christian asceticism often suffers ridicule from a general misapprehension of this truth. All the more spiritual forms of heathenism recognize the importance of the ascetic life, and in some of them it is carried to a high state of development. This is often brought forward as an argument against our christian practice; but the same might hold good against all non-christian religious sacrifices and liturgical forms of worship, which, in some Eastern systems especially, bear a striking resemblance, even in detail, to catholic christianity. There is a difference however in the underlying principle. The heathen ascetic keeps under his body either from motives of pure reason, which are good as far as they go, or (as was the case with certain of the philosophers) in order to attain to a more perfect contemplation of abstract truths. At best, heathen asceticism can only be regarded as the outcome of a feeling after God, while the christian developments of it arise from a loving desire of personal union with Him, by mystical participation in the Sacred Passion of Jesus. God never intended His creatures to suffer, He made them to be sharers of His joy: but the creature's transgression involved him necessarily in suffering, and this, Christ by His Passion has sanctified, and made a means back to joy. For the joy that was set before Him He endured the Cross. And this, and only this, must be the secret of our endurance too.

So then, we must not run into the extravagance of pretending that poverty, loss, or any kind of pain is good in itself. Christ does not say, Blessed are the poor in spirit, for they possess nothing,—but, Blessed are the poor in spirit, for theirs is the kingdom of heaven. The real beatitude of holy poverty is that it ensures us spiritual wealth. They who, for Christ's sake and the gospel's, have made themselves poor, He makes rich.

It is a matter not of total loss, as some would say, but of glorious exchange. We give up earth that we may gain heaven, and we have our Lord's sure promise that, Everyone that hath forsaken houses, or brethren, or sisters, or father, or mother, or children, or lands, for His Name's sake, shall receive an hundredfold now in this time, houses, and brethren, and sisters, and mothers, and children, and lands, with persecutions, and in the world to come eternal life.

Does it not make you smile, sisters, when people talk pityingly of the sacrifice of the religious life? I do not speak here of the evangelical poverty which is to be practised by us in the world, since for the most part it is of a kind which escapes general notice. But when one enters religion, it is generally this giving up of external possessions that mostly strikes people. Not to have any longer the disposal of one's own property, not to have indeed, strictly speaking, anything that can be called one's own at all, seems to them to be a cause for true commiseration. To have to ask for everything that one wants, even for postage stamps, is a degree of humiliation which nothing surely ever could compensate! To be clothed, fed, and housed at the expense of the community, would be, they think, sufficiently degrading; but to have the principle of poverty carried into all the trivial details of every-day life, appears an additional and quite uncalled-for degradation. In this fashion the world talks; and in so doing it patronizes, pities, and condemns those who, for Christ's sake and at His call, embrace the state of religious poverty.

In this fashion, no doubt, the friends of the young man would have talked, if, instead of going away sorrowful, he had taken our Lord's counsel, " Sell whatsoever thou hast, and give to the poor." More than eighteen centuries have passed, and the estimate which the world takes of divine things remains unchanged. The cross of Christ is still foolish, and Christ crucified is still a stumbling-block to those who know not the wisdom of God. So of religious poverty: people know not whether to pity or to scorn it most. Let those who are called to it rejoice and be glad; the world's contempt for them is a testimony that they are Christ's disciples, not in name only, but in deed and in truth.

" As poor, yet making many rich; as

having nothing, and yet possessing all things" (2 *Cor.* vi. 10). In these words St. Paul gives us a kind of epitome of the principle of evangelical poverty. This poverty, as we have seen, is more apparent in the religious state than in the secular, but it may be quite as perfect in the latter; and the reward of evangelical poverty is not restricted to either. *Everyone* that hath left all for Christ's sake shall receive an hundredfold. We know how we may voluntarily become poor, even while remaining, in obedience to Him, in the secular state. But at present we have considered only the poverty itself; now let us think of the blessedness.

"Blessed, for yours is the kingdom of heaven." Our poverty then, makes us royal, and gives us not only a future title, but a present right to kingship; "yours *is* the kingdom of heaven." Unlike some rewards, which have to be waited for, this comes at once. With our willing poverty of earthly things, comes an immediate enjoyment of heavenly riches, and in proportion as we have nothing, we indeed possess all things. In freeing ourselves from earthly interests, we have a share in those which are divine.

They run most easily who have least to carry; and we, who for Christ's sake have laid aside everything, find ourselves, almost suddenly, in regions hitherto undreamed of; with pain we detached ourselves from earth, and now behold us bound fast to God in a joy beyond words to describe! We thought we were making ourselves poor for Christ's sake, but we never knew till now what it is to be rich : for what were the houses and lands of earth compared with the kingdom of Heaven?

He shall receive an hundredfold now in this present time. Who that has taken Jesus at His word has not found it to be most blessedly true? And yet, sisters, these divine riches that come to us as the reward of our voluntary poverty are better felt than described. We should soon get landed in the regions of mystical theology—regions altogether beyond us at present—if we were to try to put into words what is meant by those "houses and lands" which are to be ours "in this present time." But we may at least say that the spiritual wealth which comes to us as the immediate reward of holy poverty, is a wealth by which we are enabled to make many rich. Who that calls to mind

St. Paul the tent-maker, standing on Mars hill, and preaching the gospel of Jesus Christ to the luxurious Athenians, does not feel that he, for all his poverty, was richer a hundredfold than they? To possess God is to possess all that belongs to God. Let us try to think out this thought for ourselves in devout meditation, and we shall be amazed at the treasure of heavenly riches which this holy poverty secures to us. We need not be afraid of claiming more than our rights, for, since we have handed ourselves over in detachment to God, He places Himself at our disposal; and it only depends upon our faith to find in Him whatsoever we desire. He is the Mine of uncreated wealth which we may search for all eternity, and never exhaust. His Wisdom, Knowledge, Power, Magnificence, Beauty, all that He is in Himself, is ours to appropriate, to delight in, to live by and to feed upon, without fear of loss or diminution or decay. Rust and moth cannot corrupt, and thieves cannot break through and steal. Unlike the treasures of earth, our heavenly treasure gives us no anxiety, being in itself abundance of peace.

Yet Christ speaks also of " persecutions '

as forming part of the present reward of holy poverty. The " hundredfold " which we are to receive now in this present time is to be " with persecutions." Truly, if we make God our all, the world will deal unkindly with us. Nothing irritates so much as contempt, and to despise earthly things is to cast a slur upon them which they will most certainly try to revenge. There are comparatively few people who, in theory at least, would not own the propriety of making God one's all ; but as soon as the theory passes into practice it meets with a nearly universal condemnation. The person who forsakes all for Christ is condemned as a visionary, an enthusiast, possibly as a lunatic. To have really no interests but God's, is to lay one's self open to the charge of folly. Holy indifference is called apathy, and an exclusive taste for divine things, selfishness. Even when for the sake of others, and to hide grace, we fain a cheerful interest in the matters of this world, we should fail to please if the real state of our feelings were known. The truth is, sisters, that everything but the service of God is a tyranny and bondage, and when it is found out that we are bound over altogether to

Him, the world will come and revenge itself upon us in every possible way for the insult we have shown it. It will speak plausibly, and charge us with neglect of social duties; it will tell us in the face of eternal truth not only that we *can* serve God and Mammon, but that we who are living in the world *ought* to do so. It will taunt us with aiming too high, and trying to take an impossible standard; and then, as if itself divine, it will pretend to settle our vocation for us by saying, "If this is the only way in which you find it possible to save your soul, why remain in the secular state at all? the right place for such as you is a convent."

In some such form persecution is sure to come to us, if we attempt honestly and bravely to live in the midst of the world for God, and God alone. If we would only content ourselves with making Him first, we might go on peaceably enough, for that is to place Him alongside of creatures, a position which many in the world would be willing to allow Him; but to make God not only first, but all, is deemed unpardonable in any but religious. Put into plain words, this is the meaning of the persecutions we are to expect. Forewarned is forearmed. If we aim at perfection we must make ourselves poor, and poverty involves detachment, and detachment is but the reverse of the spirit of the world, which takes it as a personal insult. Hence the persecution.

Let us have patience, sisters: for some of us this will, perhaps, soon be at an end. The voice of the outer world will be forgotten in that happy day when the doors of the convent close behind us for ever, and we find ourselves by God's undeserved mercy in that place whither He shall call us; while those others of us whom His secret wisdom calls to perfection in the world, must have courage. Like the three holy children who were cast bound into the midst of the fiery furnace, we too will sing, blessing the Lord. These trials are a promised part of our reward. Christ foretold them to us, and surely we are not so foolish as to wonder that His words come true. Let us bear in mind what has been already implied, viz., that all trial is a means of conforming us to Christ. The world, then, is only doing God's work in us; and if the process be painful, it is perhaps all the more effectual. As our day our strength shall be, and grace will not fail us if we be found faithful; and if long-sustained effort helps to wear us out physically rather sooner than might otherwise be the case, that will scarcely prove, I think, a matter for regret; so let us keep a good heart, and go on our way rejoicing.

Our reward, begun in time, is to last eternally. "In the world to come eternal life." Participation, that is, in the life of the uncreated God; the same life as that into which all the redeemed shall enter, but in fuller and richer proportion. It has been truly said that God is to each soul what its choice has determined that He should be. He, Who is All in All, satisfies His creatures according to their needs. He is sight to the blind, and hearing to the deaf, joy to the sad, and rest to the weary. The Psalmist sang of this long ago. "With the holy Thou shalt be holy, and with a perfect man Thou shalt be perfect." (*Ps.* xviii. 25.) They who make God their first will find Him their best, but they who make Him supreme will find Him their All. May He be glorified for ever!

LETTER VII.

Of Evangelical Chastity, and of the Excellence of Holy Virginity.

JESUS be with you, sisters, and His Name be as ointment poured forth!

The Counsel of Evangelical Perfection which we will now consider is that of chastity. By Evangelical Chastity is meant the dedication of the body and senses, the heart and the affections, in purity to God. There are three degrees of chastity—namely, that of virgins, of widows, and of married people; of these virginity far exceeds the others, and it is almost entirely of this that we shall speak. But a few words must first be said about the chastity of widows and of the married.

In giving the preference to virginity we must beware against falling into the shocking error of those who speak of marriage as if it were wrong. It is an honourable estate, instituted of God in the time of man's innocency, signifying unto us the mystical union that is betwixt Christ and His Church That which was always honourable, Jesus Himself has sanctified, and raised to the dignity of a sacrament. In forgetting this, we degrade not only marriage, but virginity also, for that is to make virginity preferable, not to a good, but to a bad thing; let marriage be duly honoured, and we shall not be blamed for shewing the excellence of virginity. When we remember that the marriage state symbolizes the union of the Church with Christ, *i.e.* of the creature with the Creator, we shall surely not be so profane as to speak lightly of it, nor so foolish as to regard with contempt those to whom God gives this call.

But to say that a thing is good, is not to deny that something else may be better. St. Paul, in commending the practice of perfection to his Corinthian converts, makes this distinction. He says: "He that is unmarried careth for the things of the Lord, how he may please the Lord; but he that is married careth for the things of the world, how he may please his wife. There is a difference also between a wife and a virgin. The unmarried woman careth for the things of the Lord, that she may be holy both in body and in spirit; but she that is married careth for the things of the world, how she may please her husband. And I speak this for your own profit; not that I may cast a snare upon you, but for that which is comely, and that ye may attend upon the Lord without distraction" (1 *Cor.* vii.) This apostolic teaching has found an echo in the Catholic Church of all ages. It declares marriage to be good, but virginity to be better; and if it be profane to deny the sanctity of marriage, it is heretical to deny the excellence of virginity. To many, probably to all whom God calls to the married state, the grace of marriage is an absolute necessity, they could not be saved without it; but those who, like St. Paul, have obtained mercy to be faithful, may humbly rejoice in their better gift of virginal chastity.

There is, however, another degree of chastity: namely, that of widows. St. Paul, in his Epistle to St. Timothy, exhorts him to "honour widows that are widows indeed," and he then describes what he means. He says: "She that is a widow indeed, and *desolate*, trusteth in God, and continueth in supplications and prayers night and day." A "widow indeed" is "desolate," that is to say, that being now loosed from her husband, she does not seek again to be bound by earthly marriage. She withdraws from carnal pleasure, that she may diligently seek

every good work. In the early Church the elder widows were consecrated by the Bishop, with imposition of hands, to the office of deaconess, or, rather, choice was made from among those who, having attained to a certain age, were thought worthy of this dignity. Their office required them to assist at the baptism of adult women, and privately to instruct female catechumens; to visit and attend the sick, and those who were in prison for confessing the faith; and to minister privately to the needs of Christians, according to the discretion of the Bishop. Some learned men are of opinion that virgins were sometimes made deaconesses, because St. Ignatius, in his Epistle to the Church in Smyrna, salutes the "virgins that are called widows," *i.e.* deaconesses, for in no other sense could virgins be congruously called widows; and in other ancient authors mention is made of virgin-deaconesses.*
Into this number only those might be received who were above a certain age, and well approved. The age, however, was not strictly defined, nor rigidly adhered to; but the younger women were for the most part refused, as it was thought they would prove

* *Bingham's Antiquities*, bk. ii. chap. 27.

unequal to this voluntary chastity; they might promise well at first, but they would perhaps not be able to persevere. Of such St. Paul says: "When they have begun to wax wanton against Christ they will marry, having damnation because they have cast off their first faith," that is, they will grow weary of heavenly love and mystical union with Christ, and will again desire earthly love, and worldly nuptials; and of those who thus act, the Apostle judges that they are dead, while they live. Not only from Holy Scripture, and the writings of the early Fathers, but from the records of every age of the Church, we gather that there have never been wanting those who after the death of their first husband have dedicated themselves to follow Christ in evangelical chastity, perfect in its degree, but less meritorious than that of virginity. Religious chastity includes each of these degrees, for virginity is not essential to religion, though evangelical chastity is proper to that state. So also this Counsel may be observed by persons of every condition according to their vocation; not by virgins only, but also by widows, married persons, and even penitents.

The most excellent degree of chastity is that of virgins. The virgin is one who, for the love of Jesus her Lord, puts aside every earthly love, that she may consecrate herself body and soul entirely to Him. In so doing she denies herself not only things that are harmless, but those which in themselves are lawful and innocent. Virginity, in the sense in which we are considering it, means something very different from mere celibacy. One who is not at present married, but who considers herself free at any time to enter the marriage state, and is perhaps only waiting the opportunity, may be actually a virgin, but she does not possess the virtue of virginity. Her condition is not specially meritorious. Virginity, to be holy, must be voluntarily chosen for the kingdom of heaven's sake. It must be the state *preferred* before any other, not merely that which is endured or tolerated. Moreover, this preference must be given from supernatural motives. Many persons remain voluntarily unmarried for various reasons. These reasons may be allowable, or they may be very good, or even in some instances heroic, *e.g.*, to check the transmission of hereditary disease, to tend an invalid parent, to devote themselves to orphaned nephews and nieces, to follow unhindered their literary or artistic pursuits, or from a mere natural love of independence, or from disappointment arising from unrequited affection or the death of the person loved. Celibacy from any such motives does not constitute a heavenly virtue. It is not in any degree religious. A person thus acting might quite lawfully marry at any time. Holy virginity, on the other hand, is inviolable, and they who for the kingdom of heaven's sake choose this blessed state, must be ready to suffer torture, and even death, rather than lose their virginal chastity. In early christian times, a virgin who broke her faith to Christ was regarded as having committed spiritual adultery, and those who rightly estimate the blessedness of the virgin state will ever thus regard such an act.

Holy virginity is a special growth and glory of the Catholic Church. It is a virtue unknown to any sectarian form of religion, and it bears witness in all generations to the blessedness of God's choice of Mary to be His Mother. Ages before the Incarnation the Holy Ghost proclaimed to His chosen people the sign by which redemption should begin, "Behold, a virgin shall conceive," and ever since the fulfilment of that promise faithful hearts have recognized a dedicated virgin life as one especially dear to God. In this we are encouraged by the example of our Lord Jesus Christ. Virgin-born, and Himself a virgin, He chose for Himself a virgin precursor and a virgin friend. His first martyrs, the blessed Innocents, were virgins, and so also, it is believed by many, was His great foster-father, St. Joseph.

The Counsel of holy virginity was given by Christ, in answer to a question of His disciples touching marriage. The nuptial bond was to be regarded, under the new dispensation, with far greater sanctity than under the law of Moses; and divorce, except for fornication, was henceforth forbidden. The disciples, hearing this, said unto Jesus, "If the case of the man be so with his wife, it is not good to marry." But He said unto them: "All men cannot receive this saying, save they to whom it is given. He that is able to receive it, let him receive it" (*St. Matt.* xix.)

Thus, not as a commandment, but as a counsel, virginity for the kingdom of heaven's sake was recommended by Christ as the better way. "All men," He said, "cannot receive this saying. . . . He that is *able*, let him receive it." Those are able to whom grace is given, but such grace is the reward and fruit of prayer. Holy virginity is not a mere gift, like that of miracles or prophecy: it is a virtue, which means, that it is the state selected by preference, and maintained by means of prayer, mortification, and life-long endurance. The attraction to virginity is a free grace, but the virtue of virginity is the result of correspondence to grace. "No man calleth himself," but the call given must also be "received," and some, Christ says, cannot receive it,—cannot, because they will not. The fearful, the prayerless, the pleasure loving, cannot receive it, for the virgin life is a life of sacrifice. But those who aspire to glory are not hindered by difficulties, and they who would take the kingdom of heaven, know that it must be taken by force.

This Counsel, then, is offered to many, but only those receive it who are able. To reject it when it is offered, is not simply to fall short of the highest perfection; it is at least to risk one's salvation. But to embrace the state of virginity from supernatural motives is to aspire to the closest union with God, and this can only be attained through suffering and conflict, to which all are not equal.

Let us ask, dear sisters, that we to whom this Counsel is given may obtain mercy to be faithful. Prayer and mortification are the essential conditions of the virgin life on earth. We shall have to speak of this more particularly later on; but we must remember, now and always, that we carry this treasure in earthen vessels, and that we are frailer and weaker than we can possibly imagine. The state of holy virginity is one in which divinest joys are mingled with exceeding sufferings, and we who aim high must also take care to keep ourselves very humble. In climbing mountain heights the path often runs along precipices, to fall over which would mean certain death. The traveller knows that his safety lies in looking upward towards the summit,—one downward look might prove fatal. And so with us, whose vocation to the virgin life is a call to the very heights of divine perfection. We must always be looking up to heaven, and away from earth; in this lies the secret of our perseverance, and our hope of glory; one earthward look may cost us our vocation.

For think what the call to virginity

OF EVANGELICAL CHASTITY. 93

means. It means that Jesus has set His choice upon us, that He desires us for Himself, and wills that, forsaking all other, we should cleave only to Him. We do not know why He has chosen us, but the Spirit that bloweth where it listeth has made us hear His voice. With more than human tenderness He invites us to His love. "Hearken, O daughter, and consider, incline thine ear; forget also thine own people and thy father's house. So shall the King have pleasure in thy beauty." We have seen One fairer than the sons of men, and His lips are full of grace. He speaks to us as never man spake, and He tells us that He has loved us with an everlasting love. He has called each one of us by name, " Rise up, My love, My fair one, and come away." He says that we have ravished His Heart, and the wound in His Side bears witness to His words. Then we know that He Who speaks to us is Jesus, and we give ourselves away to Him, not knowing what we are pledging ourselves to, not even caring to know, but conscious only of His amazing love, and our own great unworthiness.

After this, what can the world be to us but a barren and dry land where there is no way and no water: a place of exile, a desolate wilderness, from which we long to escape! The virgin soul that finds it otherwise has no true sense of her vocation; for the world has nothing in common with Jesus, and nothing that has not to do with Jesus can be of any interest to her. Unless this is the case with ourselves, sisters, we have great cause to fear. "The virgin careth for the things of the Lord," and for nothing else. Our love must be exclusive; if we attempt to let anything share our heart with Him, He will withdraw from us, for He has placed His mark upon our face, that we should admit no other lover than Himself.

No wonder, then, that holy virginity looks with desire towards the cloister, and that the virgin of Christ has a longing to enter the courts of the Lord. The religious state offers a sanctuary which nothing else can give. It encloses, supports, and protects. In the world around us there is neither enclosure, support, nor protection. Yet this is just what we seem to need, and are we to blame if we desire it? They are blessed who dwell in God's house, continually praising Him, and we would share that blessed-

OF EVANGELICAL CHASTITY. 95

ness. If virgin souls are as lilies in God's sight, religious communities may be compared to beds of lilies where He delights to feed. Here in the world we are among thorns, which would be unbearable except that they remind us of His Passion. We are alone in the wilderness, and long for companionship. "Thou that dwellest in the gardens, the companions hearken to Thy voice," cause us to hear it!

To some of us, perhaps, the call will soon come. Jesus will cause us to hear His voice, He will lead us to the flocks of His companions, and in the security of the cloister we shall be free to give ourselves altogether to the exercises of divine love. That will be a happy day, my sisters, and well worth waiting for; but the mere fact of our having to wait shews that we are not ready for it yet. Let us use well the present time, and so prepare ourselves for the joy that is in store for us. Love is very ingenious, and can convert almost anything into opportunities of grace. Let nothing baffle us, nothing dishearten us. The amiable importunities of friends, the petty tyrannies of society, the cold criticisms of the world, all that vexes or displeases in our present life, will only increase our longing for the state to which we aspire; and all longing that is patient is sanctifying too. Meanwhile, we are safe if we keep true to our vocation. Already each one of us, who for the kingdom of heaven's sake has dedicated herself in holy virginity to Christ, may say, with reverence and godly fear, "My Beloved is mine, and I am His."

But if to others of us the call to holy religion never comes, what then? Is our virginal sacrifice less dear to God? Is Jesus less truly our Beloved? Is our dedication to Him merely fictitious or imaginary, is our vocation itself a dream? There are those who in good faith will tell us so; and what wonder? They are only fulfilling the words of Christ, that "All men cannot receive this saying." Let God be true, and every man a liar: we *have* received it, for it has been given to us; and though seemingly we have our portion in this world, we know Whose we are, and to Whom we have given our love. For His virgins whom He keeps in the world, Christ prepares a dowry of special suffering which none but they can know. Passing through the vale of misery they use it for a well; and they go from strength to strength, until before the God of gods appeareth every one of them in Sion. We ourselves, sisters, might not have chosen thus, but since the choice belongs not to us, but to our Lord, let us say to Him with the holy Virgin of virgins, "Be it unto me according to Thy word."

"Blessed Agnes, standing in the midst of the flames, with outstretched hands prayed, I call upon Thee, O Father most worshipful, Father most awful; because by Thy holy Son I have escaped the threats of the wicked tyrant, and passed with unspotted foot through the foulness of the flesh; and lo! I come to Thee Whom I have loved, Whom I have sought, Whom I have always desired." *

So may we, whom God purifies for Himself in the furnace of this world, have our portion both here and hereafter with the virgins who follow the Lamb whithersoever He goeth. To Him be praise for ever!

* Antiphon for the feast, Jan. 21.

LETTER VIII.

Of the Virginal Sacrifice.

THE state of holy virginity, my sisters, does not of itself ensure our salvation; it is the means whereby we who are called to it may work out our salvation most acceptably to God, but not most easily to ourselves. In aspiring to this highest mystical union with Christ as His spouse, the soul begins a warfare against the flesh which must be painful, persevering, and life-long. This is the meaning of the virginal sacrifice, and what this implies we will now try very carefully to understand.

The call to holy virginity comes to us as an invitation from the King: "Hearken, O daughter, and consider, incline thine ear; forget also thine own people and thy father's house. So shall the King have pleasure in thy beauty." Our own people and our father's house, all that we naturally love and cling to, must be forgotten. In proportion as we dismiss from our heart and mind all merely natural affections, we shall become beautiful in the sight of God. This does not mean that we are to be cold or callous, but

OF THE VIRGINAL SACRIFICE. 99

simply that all our affections are to be supernaturalized and made divine. We are to love God supremely, and are to forget and dismiss all other loves; we are to leave father and mother, and cleave unto Him, that we may be made one spirit with Him. We that are Christ's must crucify the flesh, with the affections and desires.·

This death to nature is not easy. To all it must mean suffering, to some it will be a very martyrdom. Yet we must set ourselves to accomplish it, for so, and only so, shall the King have pleasure in our beauty. And since it has pleased His Majesty to desire us for Himself, surely there is nothing that we would not willingly do or suffer to prepare ourselves for Him? As a bride adorneth herself for her husband, so must we make ourselves ready for the Bridegroom of our souls, not counting cost, nor sparing pain; for this ·preparation, this making ready, involves both pain and cost, and these so great, that nothing less than a supernatural charity will be found equal to them. Let us pray, sisters, that the love of Christ may so constrain us, that we may be able to persevere in our holy vocation to the end. Many are called, but few are chosen; may we, in spite of all unworthiness, have grace to be found among the few!

"The kingdom of heaven is likened unto ten virgins, which took their lamps and went forth to meet the Bridegroom. And five of them were wise, and five were foolish. They that were foolish took their lamps, and took no oil with them. But the wise took oil in their vessels with their lamps."

By the oil, we may understand that special unction of the Holy Ghost without which the virgin life is impossible. Virginity is the consecration of the body and spirit to God, the appropriation to sacred uses, of all the senses and faculties, exterior and interior. As the wife hath no power over her own body, so the body of the virgin must be offered altogether to Christ. She must have no eyes but to see Him, nor ears but to hear Him, nor tongue but to speak to Him, nor heart but to love Him, nor life but for a sacrifice to Him. So, too, of her spirit; all her faculties of mind must be employed in the understanding of His Truth, the contemplation of His Beauty, the admiration of His Power. Her memory will feed on the mysteries of His Passion, her imagination will find His likeness in all good and lovely things; with her hopes she will aspire to Him; with her affections she will possess Him.

Do these words strike any of you as figurative, my sisters? At least, they represent very sober facts; but those who find them meaningless had better put this book aside. It is not meant for them, and it will do them no good. Let every one that readeth understand.

This dedication of body and spirit in virginal chastity to God is the work of the Holy Ghost. He is the blessed unction from above wherewith we are to be anointed. The work is His, but it is to be ours also. We are fellow-workers with God; "the wise virgins took the oil," the foolish virgins did not take it; there was enough and to spare for all, they might have taken it if they had willed. They failed of their calling, and were shut out from the marriage feast simply on account of their folly and negligence.

This is a very frightening thought, but a wholesome one, for I think that some of us need frightening—we are so careless, so unwilling to take pains to respond to our vocation. When we think of the favour our Lord has shown us, and the dignity to which He will raise us, ought we not to blush at the little we do to make ready for Him? If the espousals of earth are prepared for with thought and diligence, how ought not we to prepare ourselves who are so specially called to the heavenly marriage.

The married woman careth for the things of the world, how she may please her husband; she consults his wishes, studies his tastes, obeys his orders, and strives in all possible ways to be like-minded with him. And we who are betrothed to Christ must care only for such things as please Him. We must learn of Him, for He is meek and lowly of heart. We must purify ourselves as He is pure. He pleased not Himself, and neither must we. He came not to be ministered unto, but to minister, and we must be servants for His sake. He gave His life a ransom for many, and we must be willing to lay down our life for Him. Before we can be ready to go in with Him to the heavenly marriage we must be clothed with His righteousness, the beauty of the Lord must be upon us, and we must have the mind of Christ.

But how is all this to be brought about, where is this righteousness, wisdom, and beauty to be found, and what books shall we get to teach us? With the Holy Spirit for our teacher, we shall do very well with those three books that are within the reach of all, the book of nature, the book of Scripture, and the crucifix. A simple heart will best learn God in these, and simple hearts are those who learn Him best. This is one of the joys of Jesus for which He specially thanks the Father: "I thank Thee, O Father, Lord of heaven and earth, because Thou hast hid these things from the wise and prudent, and hast revealed them unto babes. Even so, Father, for so it seemed good in Thy sight" (*St. Matt.* xi. 25). We must become as little children, knowing nothing, having no preconceived ideas, no prejudices, and no fancies; willing to learn by degrees, just so much as it pleases God to teach us, and putting into practice each lesson as we learn it.

In the religious state all this would be made easier for us; for the express object of the noviciate is the training of the soul in the supernatural life. Novices are not left to themselves, as we seem to be: their mistress is always at hand to direct and admonish, to rebuke, to comfort, and to cheer. How often we in the world are tempted to wish for a novice-mistress! I say tempted, because it is always in our weakest moments that we feel this longing. The words of the eunuch then rise to our lips: "How can I, except some one guide me?" It pleases God sometimes to send us another St. Philip, whom He enlightens to give us just the help that we want at the moment, but the help at best will be only occasional. We need not on this account despond, only let us be strong and very courageous, and with prayer all will be well.

"Ask and it shall be given you, seek and ye shall find, knock and it shall be opened unto you." If we have faith to take our Lord at His Word, we shall know it to be true. The secrets of the heavenly life may be learnt by all who will. We know this, sisters, well enough; when we write it down it looks a commonplace, when we say it it sounds a mere truism. But have we ever proved it for ourselves? We must if we aspire to perfection; and when we do, it will come to us like a special revelation.

The secret of success in prayer is twofold. It must be faithful and persevering. We must believe that God will refuse no good gift to those who ask Him; and then we must go on praying till He gives it. I speak of course only of spiritual gifts, for we must lose all anxiety about temporal things. If only we would be simple and childlike in our prayers, and ask in our own words for what we want, we should not be the timidly nervous Christians that we are. When we remember our vocation, and that in stooping to ask our love, our Lord has placed Himself and all His grace entirely at our disposal, what good thing can there be that we may not ask for? I believe that no prayer, however bold, if humbly made, and with a view not to our glory, but to His, would meet with His disapproval. Elias, a man like other men, a great and fiery heart, full of passionate aches and yearnings, waited and prayed for rain; and the rain came at his request, and the parched earth yielded fruit. Such prayer, such patience, might still be found availing. Oh! for some now to pray in the spirit and power of Elias! Who would think, to judge by our feeble prayers, that the God with Whom we have to do is the very same Lord God as his?

Let the groundwork of our virgin life, then, dear sisters, be laid in prayer. If we do not know at all how to pray we must turn to our crucifix. It will teach us sooner than anything else. The Psalms of David will come to have a new meaning for us, as we hear Jesus praying them on our behalf. All the Scriptures are concerning Him, and only He can open our understanding that we may understand them. By the secret illuminations of the Holy Spirit the virgin of Christ is adorned and made ready for her Crucified Spouse. He takes of the things of Jesus, and shows them unto her, and as she beholds she herself is changed into His likeness.

The life of prayer must be continual. The apostolic precept is, "Pray without ceasing," and, though we do not live in apostolic days, let us never forget that we live in the apostolic Church. Unceasing prayer, continual recollection in the presence of God, is quite possible even in this busy age. To the virgin life it is an absolute necessity. This does not mean that we are to be continually on our knees praying (though the longer we can be on our knees the better), but only that our minds and hearts are to be always in a prayerful attitude. This will not be difficult if we really love our Lord supremely, for our thoughts naturally revert to the object of our love. Where our treasure is, our heart will be; and if Jesus be our Treasure, our heart will always be with Him. The book of nature shows forth the power, the glory, and the mightiness of His visible kingdom, just as the crucifix reveals the mysteries of His kingdom of grace. Even the coarse, rude things of the world serve by contrast to set forth His exceeding beauty. So nothing can separate us from the love of Christ; for we are always with Him.

The prayerful soul naturally loves solitude; and since the virgin life is above all a life of prayer, we must seek as much as possible to be alone. I say as much as possible, because so long as we are living in the world we shall be obliged more or less to mix with others. Here lies one of our greatest trials, which only increases as time goes on. We are tossed and baffled on every side; on the one hand we have certain social duties to perform, which for the sake of our friends we cannot omit, while on the other hand we know that we must never for a moment lose sight of our Lord, Whose rights over us are exclusive. In such matters we shall often have to make a stand, for society is very tyrannical, and can make slaves of us without our being the least aware of it. When called upon to make a stand it should be done with prudence, but if we err let it be on God's side, and not on the world's. We who have dedicated ourselves to Christ must have as little as possible to do with society, and I think it may be safely said that no one except our parents has any authority to command us in such matters. We should be free to devote ourselves altogether to an earthly spouse, and yet what would be his claims over us compared with those of our Lord? It is the privilege and the prerogative of virgins that they may attend upon the Lord without distraction. It is the only right which we have not resigned, and the only one for which we may lawfully contend.

Let us withdraw then as much as possible from all intercourse with creatures, that we may give ourselves continually to prayer. Society visits (except in obedience to parents) and all frivolous gatherings should be shunned, for they are full of secret poison, and if indulged in are soon apt to become a pleasure. Such things should be hateful to the virgin of Christ; she may be called upon to endure them, but if she takes pleasure in them she can have no true sense of her vocation. If exterior solitude is impossible, and charity requires that we should mix with others, we must at least make a solitude in our souls, and there entertain ourselves with our Lord. Let us comfort ourselves with the fifty-seventh and the hundred and twenth-third Psalms; or, since God loves importunate prayer, let us say in the words of David, "One thing have I desired of the Lord, that will I seek after; that I may dwell in the house of the Lord all the days of my life, to behold the beauty of the Lord, and to enquire in His temple;" and, having placed our cause in His hands, let us be content.

But prayer is not the only condition of the virgin life. There must also be mortification. Mortification is of two kinds,— exterior of the body, and interior of the spirit. The flesh must be crucified, with the affections and lusts. Both are necessary, for interior mortification by itself is impossible, and exterior mortification alone is useless. We dedicate ourselves body and spirit to Christ, and both must be mortified in order that we may live.

Let us be quite clear on this point.

Bodily weakness does not excuse us from bodily mortification. Unless we keep under our bodies, and bring them into subjection, they will keep us under, and will subdue us. St. Paul points out this principle when he tells us to yield our members as instruments of righteousness unto God. Our bodies are to be sanctified by the putting to death of all fleshly impulses, so that they may become helps, not hindrances, in the way of holiness. Here I speak only of such ordinary self-discipline as is within the reach of all, and could do no one any harm. This kind of mortification is absolutely necessary, and indeed holds a chief place in the virginal sacrifice. Take, for instance, the sense of sight. The virgin's eyes must be carefully guarded, not only from sinful objects, but even from things that in themselves may be perfectly good and innocent, if by looking at them her thoughts will be drawn away from Christ. She must remember that the things that are seen are temporal, but the things that are not seen are eternal; and since she is to care only for the things of the Lord, she must not willingly be taken up, even for a moment, with those of the world. Let us act upon this, my sisters, and see what it will do for us. If we make it a rule never to indulge the sense of sight in looking at merely secular objects, except when required to do so by duty or charity, we should soon find ourselves more entirely at our Lord's service. This discipline of the eyes need not at all times be exercised towards the beauties of the natural world, for God made these things for His pleasure, and what pleases Him may well please us. Nature is God's fair illuminated book, which it would be rude and ungracious, and so at least imperfect, not to delight in.

Then, too, there must be discipline of the tongue. We must learn to speak little, and to say wisely what has to be said. Our lips must be held as it were with a bridle, and our speech must be always with grace. We shall cease to lay ourselves out to please others in conversation, in proportion as we learn to discipline our tongue. This will no doubt cost us some measure of popularity, but we shall hardly regret that if it helps to deepen our union with Jesus. By degrees we shall find ourselves becoming more silent, not from moroseness, but from a habit of always listening for the voice within us, the voice of our Beloved. When we speak it will be because something has to be said, but we shall be better pleased when we need say nothing. Our tone must be gentle, our expressions modest, and we must avoid anything like exaggeration. Our laughter must not be excessive, nor our mirth uncontrolled. " A fool lifteth up his voice with laughter; but a wise man doth scarce smile a little " (*Eccles.* xxi.) If we have the grace of continual recollection this will not be difficult, but, unless we have, it will require a constant and persevering effort. All this comes by degrees, and it is the result of prayer and a childlike attention to our Lord. We catch the ways of those with whom we live : let us so carry in our hearts the image of Jesus, that our whole life may bear upon it the impress of His likeness.

Next as to the sense of hearing. It may be disciplined in many ways, especially by restraining our natural curiosity to hear news. Everything should be dull to us, unless in some way or other it has to do with Jesus; but this need not make us narrow-hearted, for His interests are wider than we often think. If *e.g.* we are obliged to listen to gossip, or even to scandal, a little ingenuity will find in it matter for intercession, or reparation, either of which would at once bring us into most intimate union with our Lord. It has been well said, that kind listening is often a most delicate act of interior mortification, it depends upon the talker that it is not an act of exterior mortification too.

Again, every sort of luxury is utterly opposed to the spirit of virginal chastity. Let us beware then of fastidiousness in food, and of the habit of eating or drinking except at meal times. It is often the truest self-denial to take the food which comes first, and not to make an invariable rule of choosing what we like least. The grand thing is to be indifferent in all such matters; and so to mortify our taste that we cease to have preferences. Our sense of smell should be denied artificial perfumes, and anything like toilet fancies. Forgive me, sisters, for speaking plainly, but in these days of cheap luxury we must learn to make our self-discipline very practical. Remembering the wormwood and the gall, how shall the virgin of Christ allow herself the use of anything that ministers, however innocently, to sensuous pleasure? The same applies to every kind of softness and ease: all delicacy must be put away, and we must accustom ourselves (as far as our state allows) to what is plain and simple. At least we must not desire luxuries. Without going into details which might not equally suit all, let me say that if we are in earnest with ourselves, and are true to our vocation, we shall become more and more in love with the cross, and shall find endless ways of signing it invisibly upon everything that we touch. Such simple habits as kneeling erect without any support; never lounging in easy positions; not allowing oneself to sit cross-legged, however tired one may be; not putting one's elbows on the table; nor fidgetting with one's hands; keeping household times with punctuality, rising early, and so on; trivial as they are in themselves, if formed with an interior motive, might become very sanctifying, and would have a special use in preparing for the religious state those of us who may be called to it.

Lastly, as to dress. Here great discretion must be exercised, and some latitude given. Speaking generally, however, let us avoid singularity, dress quietly in dark colours, and dispense with jewels and ornaments.

Our adorning should be that of a meek and quiet spirit, and, so long as we remain in the world, an unobtrusive secular dress is more likely than any other to secure for us that hiddenness which is the truest safeguard of our vocation.

Let all our things be done with charity, and, above all, let us be simple. Many very excellent people make themselves really offensive to others by their pompous fidgets about religion. Indeed, my sisters, we must beware of this. If only we will be quite child-like, and take Jesus for our model, and be natural (to use a paradox) in our supernatural following of Him, we shall be happily saved from the self-consciousness which lies at the root of this error. What is specially needed among us is an ascetic spirit which shall be both gracious and graceful; a stiff piety will never do the work that is waiting to be done. But we must be equally on our guard against laxity; and it is difficult, you say, to be uncompromising and attractive at once. No doubt; yet that is precisely what perfection enables us to be, and after all, it is no new dilemma in which we find ourselves; every one, in every age, who has aspired to be perfect, has had to face it; we are no exceptions. In quietness and in confidence shall be our strength; and if sometimes we make mistakes (as we certainly shall), our friends will perhaps forgive us, and even if they do not our Blessed Jesus will. May He be glorified in us for ever!

LETTER IX.

Of the Virginal Sacrifice. (2.)

THE sacrifice of the virgin life, as we have seen, is twofold. It is a death to our whole nature, both exterior and interior. By exterior mortification we must subdue the body, and offer it to God; and by interior mortification the spirit also must be subdued, and offered to Him. The two must go together, or the sacrifice will be incomplete. It is the fashion in these days to make much of the last, and to deny the importance of the first. Considering that mortification of the body strikes at the root of comfort, and that comfort is our great national idol, this is not surprising. But what analogy does comfort bear to the crucifix? and if it bears none, what ought we to have to do with it? The truth is that our natural spirit is carnal, and can only be got at through the flesh. This must be attacked and subdued before our spirit can ever be really mortified. St. Paul, who, with the exception of our Blessed Lord Himself, is the greatest ascetic teacher the world has ever seen, leaves no doubt upon this point. He says, "If ye do mortify the deeds of the body ye shall live." The life of the spirit then, according to apostolic teaching, depends upon this very mortification of the body which is so despised. We hear a good deal of talk about "Pauline theology;" would that we might see something of Pauline practice!—the perishing of the *outward* man; "always bearing about in the *body* the dying of the Lord Jesus" (2 *Cor.* iv.); the *body* a living sacrifice; "in necessities, in stripes, in watchings, in fastings." (2 *Cor.* xii.) These are not the words of a mediæval mystic, but the sober language of an Apostle; and whatever other Christians may have to say to them, the virginal sacrifice, my sisters, requires that we should understand them as facts of our own experience.

But this exterior mortification is a means only; the end is mortification of the spirit. Our whole being must die, that it may live;

we must be made one spirit with Jesus, as He Himself is one with God. Our nature, like the grain of wheat, cannot bring forth fruit except it die; and it is our Lord's most earnest desire that we should bring forth fruit. There must be then, first of all, a putting to death of our natural spirit, in order that it may be made supernatural and fruitful. We must cease to be what we naturally are; and must supernaturally become what naturally we are not. Pride must be put to death, that it may rise humble, and covetousness must be mortified till it becomes liberality. Eagerness must wear the bonds of patience, and sloth be scourged into fervour, and self-will crucified into obedience. We must voluntarily destroy all that we know ourselves to be by corrupt nature, that we may be created anew by the Holy Spirit of God in the likeness of Jesus.

In order to do this we must study Him. We cannot learn anything without study, we cannot grow into the image of the Crucified, unless we give ourselves to meditation on the Passion. This was the practice of the saints, by means of which they became what they were; and if we hope ever to attain to perfection, this must be our practice too. "The excellency of the knowledge of Christ Jesus" is best learnt in the words of the Holy Ghost Himself. Gospel commentaries, useful as they may be, are not to be compared with the actual Gospel; so also no book of meditation on the Passion comes near the beauty of the Passion itself. Let us ask God to make a silence in our hearts, and to let that silence be unbroken, except by the voice of the Holy Ghost. "The Comforter," Christ said, shall teach you, "for He shall take of Mine, and shall shew it unto you." (*St. John* xvi.)

Let us ask, then, to be shewn the things of Jesus the Lamb. We who are virgins are especially called to follow Him whithersoever He goeth ; and by this following we are to understand the interior sacrifice of the spirit, the offering of our whole being to Him. Our habits of mind, our tastes, our general view of things, must be formed on the model of the "Lamb slain." As He was offered without spot to God, so we must be presented to Him, having neither spot, nor wrinkle, nor any such thing. We must purify ourselves even as He is pure.

First, then, there must be purity of intention. The true virgin of Christ seeks in all things the glory of her heavenly Spouse. She knows that He looks not so much at what is done, as at the way in which it is done, and the motive for doing it. Just as the refiner looks into the molten gold, and sees himself reflected there, so Jesus looks into the virgin's life and finds His image in all her actions. Common things become divine that are done in the spirit of Jesus, and for the love of Him. Holy virginity takes the good savour of Christ everywhere, being itself penetrated with His sweetness. Life ceases to be drudgery and becomes worship, when we remember for Whom we are living, and Who it is Who has set His Love upon us, and that we are no longer our own but His. This is what makes our detention in the world endurable. If only we keep bravely to our present duty, we can make some corner of this wilderness bright for Him, and if this is His choice for us, we will gladly make it our own, and not disappoint Him by a heavy-hearted service that can never glorify Him. So too, if He gives us the grace of a cloistered life, let it be His glory, not our own sanctification, that we keep most in view. For all glory is

His, and our only glory is this, that we glorify Him.

Next comes purity of desire. As the earthly spouse seeks to please her husband, so the virgin of Christ must be always looking to her Lord, desiring only those things that are pleasing in His sight. When a choice has to be made she will not consult her own wishes, nor do the easiest thing, nor the thing which will win her most praise. She will turn to Jesus Crucified, saying, "Lord, what wouldst Thou have me to do?" and when she knows His will, she will gladly do it in the happiness of pleasing Him. If it costs her much it will only be that He is putting her love to the test; not because He doubts it, but because, knowing all things, He knows that she loves Him well enough to endure suffering for His sake.

Then there must be purity of affections. The dross of earthly loves must be purged away; there must be no clinging to creatures, no sharing of the heart with them. When the love of Christ constrains us to follow Him in holy virginity, there must be an end to every human love that is not also divine. Henceforth know we no man after the flesh; all carnal love, even that which is in itself right and innocent, becomes an impossibility for us. Human familiarities must be avoided, for our bodies are consecrated to God; all caresses and strong terms of endearment must cease, for we have given ourselves altogether to Jesus. No one has any right over us now but He; for we are virgins, and the virgin's heart is made over to Him, that she may be able to say, with the spouse in the Canticle, "I am my Beloved's, and my Beloved is mine! His left hand is under my head, and His right hand doth embrace me; let Him kiss me with the kisses of His mouth." If we have truly tasted the blessedness of our vocation, sisters, we shall know that the soul that hath Jesus desires no carnal love, and we shall shrink from human tendernesses, except when it is our duty to endure them, like other sufferings, for His sake.

Lastly, every thought must be chastened and made a pure offering to God. There is work to last a life-time here, and one which we may think ourselves happy if we ever complete on this side the grave. Thoughts are deeds; and they are by far the most numerous of our deeds, for there is never a moment, except when we are asleep, that we are not thinking. Our thoughts give the tone to our words and actions, and help more than either of these to form our character. Not only so, but each separate thought does its own work in us, and tends either to develope or to destroy the divine life of the soul. Thoughts create an interior atmosphere, in which grace will either thrive or languish. They may never pass into words or actions, yet they are always busy doing their work. Every thought that has ever found a place in our heart will meet us again at the last day; for God will judge the secrets of men, and He is a discerner of thoughts. The virgin consecrates her thoughts to God, and nothing that defileth is allowed for one moment to find entrance into her soul, for she knows that her Beloved is of too pure eyes to behold iniquity, and that since they are continually upon her she must be chaste in spirit as in body. He understands her thoughts long before, and He desires that they should be a reflection of His own. She will, therefore, only allow herself to think of things that are true, honest, just, pure, lovely, and of good report. If there be any virtue, and if there be any praise, she will think on these things; but all that ministers to strife, envy, discord, or vexation, she will put aside as unprofitable, since they do not bear upon them the image of her Spouse. She will be happiest when her thoughts can be directly of Him, but she will never be unhappy, for they will never be far off Him.

The habit of frequently making acts of love to our Blessed Lord is perhaps the surest and easiest way of purifying our thoughts. It is a simple habit, that can soon be formed, and in itself it is so delightful that nothing short of the Sacraments can compare with it. If you do not know this already, my sisters, may He give you grace to believe what I say; for I am sure that there is nothing more sanctifying. Whenever there comes a pause in our thoughts, let us fill it with an act of love to our good Jesus; and let it come naturally, in our own words, as if He were really present with us, as indeed He is. This habit in itself, if persevered in, would take us a great way towards perfection, and, as I have said, it is so delightful that perseverance will be found quite easy. It will make our hearts like thuribles, in which the holy fire is always burning; and it may be that one of the reasons why our Lord keeps us in the world is that we may go about breathing acts of love, and so making it, in spite of itself, fragrant as with incense for Him. This will strengthen us, perhaps, when we are tempted to wish ourselves elsewhere as who that loves is not, at times? But, remember, it is a temptation, and we must not indulge in it; for when He wants us elsewhere, He will most surely let us know.

By this consecration of our whole interior to God, as well as by the mortification of our body and sense, the virginal sacrifice is completed. It is not a sacrifice made once for all, it must be daily renewed and offered. Perfection means union with the Infinite, and can therefore never be attained in this life. We are to "go on unto perfection," and we must be always "going on." The separation is not accomplished at once, and the sense of separation increases every day. We are left more and more alone with God, and His Presence makes itself more intensely realized. We used to fear death, but gradually the fear lessens, and sometimes, though perhaps not in our bravest moments, we find ourselves longing for it.

Yet it will hardly be a new thing when it comes, for we are beginning to know what St. Paul meant when he said, "I die daily." When most mixed up with the world we often feel already dead, for we are crucified to it, and are only waiting to be taken down from the cross, which seems to have done its work, though this cannot really be the case, or God would take us down from it. We are dead, and our life is hid with Christ; we seem really to live only when we are at our prayers, all the rest is little better than dying.

"Dying, and behold we live!" Here is the secret joy of our virginal sacrifice. Actually short of God Himself, Whom we shall possess as our reward, there is no joy to be compared with the life of mortification. It is the conscious putting off of mortality that we may be clothed with immortality. There is pain indeed, and suffering, but they are nothing in respect even of present joy. It cannot be put into words, for there are no human words to express it. It is a joy with which no stranger can intermeddle; a peace which no man taketh from us. It is the very joy of heaven itself, begun in time as the recompense of the offering of our

OF THE VIRGINAL SACRIFICE.

virginal chastity to God. It is a [...]
that passeth understanding, by whi[ch...]
already begin to enter into union wi[th our]
Lord.

And for this joy, and this peace, w[e must]
not go to the cloister : holy virgini[ty can]
live and flourish among the thorns [of the]
world. The Lord knoweth them th[at are]
His, and He can keep them from t[he evil]
and purify them for Himself. Beca[use we]
have set our love upon Him, theref[ore will]
He deliver us.

Our sacrifice will cost us someth[ing, dear]
sisters, it would not be a sacrifice [if it did]
not ; but when things go hardly wit[h us, let]
us take refuge with our crucifix, and, [kneeling]
down before it, say, each one for her[self, It]
is Jesus Whom I love, I am bec[ome the]
spouse of Him Whose Mother was a [Virgin,]
and Who was begotten spiritually [by the]
Father, of Him Whose sweetes[t name]
sounds already in mine ears. If I [love Him]
I am chaste, when I touch Him I [am pure,]
when I possess Him I am a vir[gin. To]
Him be praise for ever !

LETTER X.

Of the Joys of Holy Virginity.

often true, my sisters, as we saw in the last to it, that the joy of our virginal sacrifice from the nd words to describe; but that is no work, the why we should not be able to speak or God in things which belong to this way of dead, which indeed form part of its conditions, seem reich are in themselves as fountains of prayers, the virgin soul. When we look back that has already been said, perhaps

"Dyinus may be afraid that this sacrifice is the sad our strength, although, when we Actually consider it in detail, there is nothing shall posieroic in what we have to do! No to be com been laid down as to fasts and It is these; nor any allusion made to those that we inary penances and mortifications There is to read of in the lives of the saints. are nothive been purposely omitted, for two It cannot ple reasons: first, because we are no human saints, and secondly, because these with which ll not of themselves ensure our peace whic

the very join is not arrived at by extra. as the rec but by ordinary means; at least this is mostly the case. We are beginners, and for the present we must content ourselves with small things; let us be ingenious, humble, and persevering in our petty mortifications, and see what robust, and practical, and cheerful Christians we may soon become! Unless this "daily dying" produces in us a great interior joy, there must be something seriously wrong in our method; if it saddens and depresses us, we have probably altogether mistaken our vocation, a thought which we will not dwell upon in this place. However hard and impossible the virginal sacrifice may seem to be in theory, those who are called to make it will find it delightful in practice; and these letters are for such as are called, and not for others.

So much concerning the sacrifice; and now for the joys of the virgin life. They are so many, and so great, that we must be prepared, sisters, for a long letter, which, considering the subject, will require no great patience on our part.

The solid basis, the foundation joy, of holy virginity consists in God's choice of, and union with, the soul. To be the object of choice, and of such a choice! To know that not an earthly, but a heavenly Lover

K

has set His Heart upon us, and that He desires to espouse us to Himself in an eternal and mystical union of the highest degree, is a joy which must be known to be felt. The joy of earthly espousals only faintly signifies this. The difference is the difference between that which is human, and that which is Divine; the joy itself is ineffable, it cannot be uttered ;

"The love of Jesus, what it is
None but His loved ones know."

Yet the cause of the joy can be partly explained; it arises from mutual attraction.

It is not hard to know why we love Jesus. He is so beautiful, that it would be impossible to know Him and not love Him. It is harder at first to understand why He loves us, until we remember that He can only love goodness, and that all goodness wherever it exists comes from Him, and is His own. The reason, then, why He loves us is that He recognises in us something that belongs to Him, something that is peculiarly His, and that He has bestowed upon us in order that we may love Him, and that He may love us, with a special unifying love, with the love of espousal.

This is in itself a most wonderful grace;

it is altogether unmerited on our part: we did nothing to deserve it in the first instance, and perhaps we have many times since proved ourselves unworthy of it. Jesus set His choice upon us, and marked us out for the virginal sacrifice, and made us dimly feel how holy a thing it might be, long before we could put the feeling into words. He jealously guarded us for Himself when, humanly speaking, the chances were all against our ever responding to our vocation; we were growing hard and cold, perhaps, from long discouragement and contact with the world, and He made us pass through fire, that we might be warmed into our right self again, and won back to our first love. He was more patient with us than any earthly lover would have been; His desire for us was so great that nothing could baffle it. He was intent upon gaining us for Himself, and all for the love of that which He Himself had given us, the undying love of holy virginity.

If such has been His desire in the past, will it be less now, when with our whole heart we have given ourselves to Him, and have pledged Him all our love? Impossible. No matter how imperfect we feel ourselves to be, so long as that promise given, that dedication made, is never for one moment regretted, we are blessedly safe. Temptations may press upon us, sin may assail us, hell itself may seem to be let loose upon us, but, "though an host of men were laid against me, yet shall not my heart be afraid, and though there rose up war against me, yet will I put my trust in Him: for I am persuaded that neither death nor life, nor angels, nor principalities, nor powers, nor things present, nor things to come, nor height, nor depth, nor any other creature shall be able to separate me from the love of God which is in Christ Jesus our Lord." (*Ps.* xxvii.; *Rom.* viii.) To some of us there may come times in our life when all seems lost: when there is a sort of universal collapse, and we are left alone with a sorrow which no earthly heart can share, in a desolation which is simply terrifying; then let us remember Whose we are, and why we are His, and how we are His, and the thought of our virginal union with Him will give us an archangel's strength, and more than an archangel's joy.

If our union with Christ ensures us His support and sympathy, it also demands that we should suffer and rejoice with Him. In His Mystical Body, the Church, Jesus is still suffering ; her passion is the filling up of His own, and just as He looked then for some to have pity on Him, so does He now. The invitation to watch and pray which He gave to His chosen in Gethsemane, is still repeated to those whom He calls to follow Him, and has a special meaning and significance for virgin souls ; for now is the hour of darkness, the hour of the Church's agony, when the prince of this world cometh, and must find nothing in her. Christ took our infirmities and bare our sicknesses, and for love of Him His faithful virgins will take home to their hearts, and make their own, the griefs and wrongs of holy Church. In all her afflictions they will behold their Lord afflicted, and by every possible means they will try to alleviate what must be endured. Let us resolve then, my sisters, to spare no pains, and to grudge no cost. Mary of Bethany has set us an example of devotion which we, at least, have a right to follow if we will. Let us pour out our very precious things upon the Church, and be assured that in so doing we are really ministering to Jesus. Men will be indignant, and even disciples will complain of waste; but He will say of us that we have wrought a good work, and His approval is all that we care for.

We must always remember that the Church's glory is to be estimated by her resemblance to her Lord. Humanly speaking He was a failure, if ever there was one, and humanly speaking the Church will be a failure too. Her portion, like His, is to "suffer, and so to enter into glory," and not only to suffer *with* Him, but in the same way that He suffered. Christ was betrayed by an apostle, and many a time those high in office will be found traitors to the Church. He was tried illegally in a secular court, by unbelieving judges, and the Church in this land and age can glory that so is she. He was condemned on false charges by men who hated the truth, and in like manner the Church must look for her condemnation. He was scourged, and arrayed in a fool's garment, and treated with derision by an ignorant rabble urged on by blaspheming priests, and so will the Church will be outraged. He trod the way of sorrows to His Crucifixion, and there is no other road along which the Church can follow Him, no other death than the death of the Cross, by which she can be conformed to the likeness of her Lord.

Who that loves Jesus with pure virginal love, will ever be impatient with the Church in her afflictions? See how beautifully she is being steeped in the glory of His Passion! She is wounded by her friends, despised, rejected, and made the very scorn of men; they that sit in the gate speak against her, and the rebukes of them that rebuked her Lord are fallen upon her. Is there no beauty here to remind us of Him? and if there is, surely we shall love her most for her very sufferings that are so Christ-like. As with Him, the waters are come in even unto her soul; she sticks fast in the deep mire where no ground is, and is come into deep waters so that the floods run over her. Like Him she can say, "I am weary of crying, my throat is dry, my sight faileth me for waiting so long upon my God. They that hate me without a cause are more than the hairs of my head; they that are mine enemies and would destroy me guiltless are mighty." (*Ps.* lxix.)

In the midst of all this suffering, the Church looks for the support and compassion of virgin souls. If we are faithful to Jesus, we shall be faithful to her. Zeal for the Church is one of the marks of the true lover of Christ; and one of the privileges and joys of our virgin life is precisely this, that we may minister to our Lord in her. The Church's affliction is but for a moment, a great weight of glory is laid up for her hereafter. In the world she will have tribulation, yet the time of her trial is also a time of special blessedness for us. With Veronica, who, as tradition tells, wiped the Face of Jesus on the road to Calvary, we may do like service for the suffering Church as she goes out to crucifixion; and the beauty of our Lord shall be upon us as the reward of our devotion.

We can plead her necessities in prayer, and offer our intentions for her at Mass, and associate others with us in intercession on her behalf. We can refrain from discussing ecclesiastical affairs, for no argument of ours will help to improve them, and we can spread the blaspheming letters of the enemy before our Lord in silence, and make acts of reparation in our hearts to Him. When persecution runs high, and we are tempted to shoot out arrows, even bitter words, let

OF HOLY VIRGINITY. 137

us seal our lips with the sweet Name of Jesus, and be as those that hear not, in whose mouth are no reproofs. In such ways we shall be invisibly doing for the Church what the Cyrenian did for Jesus, helping her to bear the cross. To hearts that love Him all this will mean joy, the joy of ministering to Him, Who Himself is always ministering to us.

But there is another kind of sympathy which the virgin life also requires of us. Hand in hand with zeal for the Church goes love for souls. It may be said to be almost the same thing under another aspect. It is impossible to be zealous for the Church without feeling an intense interest in the souls whom it is her office to save; neither can we pray much for the Church generally without coming also to pray individually for souls. Conversions are going on every day all the world over; and each conversion means a new triumph for the Church, a new glory to our Lord, and therefore a new joy to us. The prayers of virgins are a positive element in the conversion of sinners, a real help to the Church in doing her work, and an effectual means of increasing the honour of our Blessed Lord. We may thus be always lifting up the lost sheep into the arms of Jesus, Who lays them on His shoulders rejoicing; always helping to renew the joy which is so great that God seems unable to keep it to Himself, and must needs call together His friends and neighbours, saying, " Rejoice with Me." What happiness for us, sisters, to be allowed to increase and to share in the redeeming joy of our Lord over lost sinners, whom we have helped Him to save. Intercession for sinners, and prayer for the guidance and renewal of individual souls, will be one of the daily joys of our virgin life.

Those of us who can will do more than this; we shall ourselves labour actively on behalf of others. To turn many to righteousness is a glory perhaps beyond our hopes; but to help even one soul to love Jesus better is a joy worth living for. With His love warm in our hearts, a smile can win a victory for Him, which without it no words could do; and the deeper He allows us to drink of His cup of sorrow, the more freely we shall be able to pour out the oil of gladness upon the wounds of others. It is worth while to have one's own heart broken, for the capacity that it gives for binding up the hearts of others. Let us bear this in mind whenever a sorrow comes; it is meant to make us apostolic and tender-hearted, that we may the more readily bear the burdens of others, and so speed them on their way to Christ. This joy is better felt than described; it is one of those many things that will hardly bear being put into words.

A further joy of the virgin life is the result of the development within us of the likeness of our Lord. The virgin can say more truly than any other, " the life that I now live in the flesh I live by the faith of the Son of God;" for that which is natural dies, and that which is supernatural grows, and increases day by day. We are to live not only altogether for Christ, but altogether by Him. We are bone of His Bone, and flesh of His Flesh, just as we, being joined to Him, are made one spirit with Him. And so it comes to pass that we find ourselves thinking His thoughts, and falling into His ways. What was difficult a little while ago is easier now; soon it will be so easy that it will pass into a habit, and habit is second nature. We wonder how this has come about, yet the answer is not far to seek. The transforming of the natural into the supernatural can only be effected by one thing,—by faithful correspondence to sacramental grace.

May the Holy Spirit convince you, sisters, of the truth of what I say. The virgin life must be nourished by frequent sacraments, if it is to be worthy of its name and of our Lord. I speak of course to those who live within the reach of sacraments, for, if necessary, the divine love will find out ways of effecting the grace which properly belongs only to God's covenanted means. If we have a true sense of our vocation we shall never willingly omit a sacrament; we shall be regular and frequent in our confessions and communions; and since only Jesus can make us fit for Jesus we shall, whenever we can, present ourselves at the tribunal of penance before receiving the Blessed Sacrament. There we become quick-sighted to our faults, and what used to look trifles when measured by human standards, will be seen to be more serious by a standard which is divine. We shall spend less time in self-examination than formerly, yet find more matter for self-accusation, and so our confessions will come to be more spontaneous, and, what is better still, more heart-broken. This is the work of the Precious Blood. Frequent absolutions will tell upon us at last, and we shall thank God that we resisted that subtle spiritual temptation whereby the evil one sought to ruin us by hindering us from confession; for as time goes on we shall see that it has not only saved us from sacrilegious communions, but has given us a hatred of venial sin, and a tender devotion to the Passion which nothing else perhaps could have given. We go to the Altar with contrite hearts, having made our peace, and, no matter how we may feel, we know that in God's sight we are bright and warm with the Precious Blood, and that, bearing upon us this token of acceptance, we shall find a welcome from Him. Alas! for those who call themselves catholics, and yet speak as if they did not love the sacrament of Penance: surely they cannot know it as we do, or they could not talk of it so. One of the joys of our virgin life must be to spread devotion to this sacrament, and to offer reparation to our Lord for the coldness with which so many of His children regard it, as though it were an object of fear, rather than of reverent and most tender love.

But what of our communions? They are the means by which we dwell in Christ, and He in us. They are the continual ratification, and seal, and renewal of that essential joy of the virgin life, union. They are a pledge of those mystical espousals for which we long, and towards which we are hastening; the foretaste of the marriage feast to which they that are ready shall enter in. With what joy we who are virgins should receive Jesus in His Blessed Sacrament, when we remember that each communion binds us more indissolubly into union with Him, and gives us new capacities for loving, and for being loved. When we think of the dignity of our vocation, of our own unworthiness, and of the greatness of His Majesty, Who so condescends to desire us for Himself, words fail to express the wonder of the joy that He prepares for us in the Blessed Sacrament of His love.

For many of us, too, there is the joy of daily Mass. Think what it is to be allowed to spend the first hour of each day in the actual presence of our Lord. Those of us who are living in the world, and who have this privilege, can hardly imagine what life would be without it, for we can gather joy there enough to gladden ourselves and others the whole day long. To give way to gloom or depression during a day begun with Mass is dishonouring to our Lord, and damaging to our souls. It would be a good plan when we have reason to anticipate such a thing, to spend the whole of our time at Mass in making acts of joy.

The spirit of reparation, and the habit of making acts of reparation, have a wonderful power of producing joy in the soul. We live in the midst of a world in which God is ignored. The character of the age, on the whole, is indifference; men are more careless about God than at open enmity with Him. Yet carelessness, indifference, lukewarmness, is the state of all others which God most abhors; clearly then it is the one which most dishonours Him. It would be quite a revelation of the world's actual state of indifference towards God, if at some given moment a census could be taken of the thoughts of every human being now living. How many out of the millions of the earth's population are at this moment occupied with God? Yet every soul in creation was made in order that it might occupy itself with Him, and with nothing else. God then is being ignored, and defrauded of His rights, by every soul that is not at every instant more or less consciously engaged in His service; that is, certainly, by the immense majority of mankind. We can, however, do something to repair this dishonour which is being ignorantly offered to the Majesty of God; we can ourselves be perpetually making acts of love to Him on behalf of others. Thus, when we find ourselves in company, we can make an act for each person present, and offer it to our Lord, desiring that He should be known, loved, and eternally praised by all creatures, and especially by those in whose company we are. Perhaps there is no practice more pleasing to Him than this of making acts of love, which in their very nature are acts of reparation and of intercession too. It is an exercise of charity towards both God and man, which, while it ensures us a future reward, is also a present joy.

One other source of joy, and the last which we will here speak of, is that which comes from the growing experience of our Lord's fidelity to us. At first we committed ourselves to Him, not knowing what He would do with us, hardly indeed caring to know. Then came trials, the parting in spirit from friends, the gradual detachment of self from things we were clinging to, the suspicion or cold criticism of those we loved. Each step that we took meant new pain, and the answer to every prayer came through suffering. Courage would have failed us if love had faltered, but just when all seemed lost, a new power came into our soul, and took possession of us, and bore us on in spite of fears, and bound us close to Jesus. Now that we have gone a little way we can look back, and see that all that has been done in us is His doing, and that our present grace is because of His fidelity to us, rather than our fidelity to Him. We feel ourselves to have been very craven sort of lovers, and the best that can be said of us is that we have just been saved from proving false. No one but Jesus Who knows all things could have known that we have really loved Him all the while. We have doubted it ourselves sometimes, and He has re-assured us, and has bidden us take heart, and believe in His work of grace. We know that He is faithful, and each new trial as it comes only proves His faithfulness the more, for when the sorrow passes, our union with

Him breaks upon us like a fresh joy, as something which we have never realized before.

How He can love us, as we know He does, is a wonder to-day, and it will be a wonder through all eternity. Yet do we not act as if we doubted Him when we are restless, and over-anxious, and full of plans for ourselves? He keeps us in the world for His own purposes, and we can complain, as though He were making us suffer needlessly, or we grow tepid as though fervour were impossible except in the cloister. Believe me, sisters, unless we trust Him more than this, we deserve to lose our vocation altogether. So we be virgins betrothed to Christ, it matters not where we await the consummation of our espousals; enough to know that He Who has set His love upon us will do for us all that is in His Heart. Only let us desire His glory, and His joy will remain in us, and our joy shall be full. May He be praised above all for ever!

LETTER XI.

Of the beauty of Holy Virginity.

I HAVE tried to speak to you, dear sisters, of the sacrifice of the virgin life, of the sufferings which that sacrifice involves, and of the joys which are the fruit of those sufferings. Let us go on now to consider what that beauty is which our Lord desires to see in the soul that He will espouse to Himself: that we may learn by His grace how to beautify ourselves for Him.

As the earthly bridegroom rejoices over his bride, so does Christ over His virgin. He is jealous over her with godly jealousy, that she may be presented to Him having neither spot, nor wrinkle, nor any such thing. What He desires for her most of all is purity. Not only her outward works, but her innermost being must be pure; for the King's daughter is all-glorious within, and no amount of external beauty will please Him unless the heart itself is altogether pure. The virgin then, must have no mixed motives, no desire for personal distinction, nor even for individual holiness, considered as a thing by itself. Purity is a simple living for God, apart from any benefit which may result from so living. It looks at everything in the light of God, measures it by His rule, weighs it by His standard, and accepts or rejects it accordingly. Purity is a very unearthly grace; it can live in the world, but can never be of the world; it is only at home with God, but with Him it is always at its ease. It reflects His own simplicity, and gives back His likeness: it reminds Him of Himself, and is especially dear to Him on that account. It perceives truth at a glance, and loves it as its own life. It is courageous, having nothing to fear, and strong, being united to God. The pure soul has put on the Lord Jesus, and clothed herself with the snowy fleece of the Lamb. No wonder then, that beholding her, He loves her, and greatly desires her beauty.

If purity is to be the virgin's robe, humility must be her veil. She will seek to live to God in secret, and will wish only to please Him. Humility is the guardian of all other graces, for it conceals them, and keeps them for God. It shrinks from human praise, and loves to pass unnoticed. It avoids the gaze of earth, and lives quietly beneath the eye of heaven. It is content with lowly things, and would rather serve than reign. It distrusts self altogether, but entirely trusts God. It can walk safely in high places, because it goes everywhere, and does everything in His strength.

Humility is a very joyous spirit. It sings the song of Mary the Mother of God, and magnifies not itself, but Him. It is a silent spirit too, and has a way of pondering divine mysteries, and of keeping sacred things to itself. It serves the Lord with fear, and rejoices unto Him with reverence. It waits for the leadings of grace, and is never in a hurry to go on. It keeps its eye fixed on God, and is not uneasy about itself. It rests on His Wisdom, and is quite willing to seem foolish in the sight of men; it is content to be abased, that He may be exalted.

When Jesus sees a humble soul He desires her for Himself; for humility is the queen of all creaturely graces, and He can work wonders in a humble soul that He cannot work in any other. The lack of humility cost Lucifer a throne, and the grace of it won Magdalene a crown. It is essentially the spirit of Jesus, the spirit of the Incarnation, and even if without it holy virginity were possible, it would not be beautiful in His sight. The spouse of Christ must be humble as well as pure.

She must also be obedient, subject in all things to her Lord, and willing for His sake to live in subjection to others. Obedience binds the virgin soul to Christ. It glories in a captivity which is perfect freedom, and bears a yoke which is more than liberty. It emulates the angels in their service, and is eager to fulfil commands which are scarcely yet uttered. It resigns choice, and is intent upon obeying orders rather than discussing them. It honours all men for God's sake, and submits itself not only to the good and gentle, but also to the froward. It remembers how the Creator was bound with cords by His creatures, and led before an unjust judge, and it does not wish to exercise an independence which He disdained. It is content that another should gird it and carry it whither it would not. It adores the divine predestination, certain that God can work His Will and bring about His glory, as well in one way as another. It puts itself at the disposal of creatures, in order to be the more completely at the disposal of the Creator. It never finds itself in adverse circumstances, because everything that happens is subject to His ordering. It sets its face towards Calvary, and carries on its own shoulders the cross on which it is to die. When the time comes it will lie down thereon of its own free will, never so free as then, and give itself to death. The hour of sacrifice will be its hour of victory, and through death it will pass to life.

The meekness of the Passion enters into the soul of the virgin, and makes her obedient like her Lord. She follows the Lamb whithersoever He goeth, and He turns and sees her following, and loves her for the beauty that is His Own, and desires her for Himself that she may be His bride, having the glory of God.

The spouse of Christ must also be modest. Modesty is like a mantle that hides other graces. It is the one grace which appears on the surface, and which does not suffer from being seen. It is the result of a disciplined mind re-acting upon the body, and affecting the whole exterior, making it ordered and comely, just as the whole interior is moderated and controlled. Many things besides prayer are learnt in meditation, and modesty is one of these things. The virgin takes Jesus for her model, and unconsciously falls into His ways of doing even common actions. Familiarity with Him softens her voice, restrains her laughter, and refines her whole manner. She does everything as to the Lord, and the result is an habitual modesty. Whilst often gay, she is always recollected, and in patience she possesses her soul. She is quiet in the midst of joy, and calm in affliction. The tranquillity of God, with Whom is no variableness neither shadow of turning, has fallen upon her, and given her a dignity that nothing else can give. There is something very divine about modesty, especially virginal modesty. There is something royal about it too; the King Himself has pleasure in its beauty.

Faith must also shine as a bright lamp in the hand of the virgin whom Christ shall choose and receive unto Himself. It will give her confidence in the day of trial, and hope in His promises, and courage to do and to suffer great things for Him. It will teach her how to pray, and will give her understanding of mysteries, and zeal for the truth, and hatred of heresy. It will cheer her in failure, and encourage her to make new ventures for Christ. It will inspire her with loyalty to the Church, and will feed her devotion, and illuminate her intelligence, and turn all things into revelation. It will light up dark corners of the earth, and discover God everywhere. By faith the saints became what they were, and by faith she will become what her Lord desires she should be. Whatever He wills her to accomplish, faith will enable her to do; and by means of it she shall be more than conqueror through Him that loveth her.

Moreover, the virgin must be crowned with endurance, for it is not enough to begin well, she must endure to the end. Many are called, but few are chosen; and precisely for this reason, that though many can endure for a time, few can endure "to the end." Endurance is prolonged patience, a *habit* of patience, which comes from continual conscious union with God, without which, sooner or later, endurance is certain to give way. The soul that clings to creatures cannot endure, because it always fears the loss of creatures, and when it loses them it has nothing to cling to, and no one can endure *alone*. But the soul that is detached from creatures can cling with all its might to God, and the soul that clings to God can endure anything. Trials only bind her the more closely to Him, suffering only strengthens her endurance; she endures not in her own strength but in His; and she knows that in crowning her His bride, He will be crowning a beauty which He Himself has given, that He might desire it.

But the perfecting of the virgin soul is love. It was the love of Christ that constrained her at the first and bade her follow Him. It was love that shed His Blood for her, and bought her a robe of purity that she might be spotless in His sight. It was love that opened to her the depths of divine humility, and taught her how to live despised and lowly like Himself. It was love that conquered her with Christ's obedience, and led captive her soul in meekness, and put a girdle round about her, and a yoke upon her neck, and made her free indeed. It was love that covered her with modesty, and taught her how to do all things graciously, and made her royal. Love placed the light of faith in her hand, and showed her how to trim it when it burned dim, and how to walk fearlessly in its shining. Love detached her from earth, and bound her to itself, and

itself endured in her all that she suffered for
love's sake, and crowned her for enduring.
And love will be the perfecting of its own
work, and will finish what it has begun in
her, and will desire the beauty it has given
her. For Love will be to her what it is to
Itself, All in all.

Such is the beauty, dearest sisters, which
our Lord wishes to see in us, and without
which we cannot please Him. It is a beauty
altogether divine and heavenly. It cannot
be learnt by human skill, nor acquired by
human art. We can only attain to it in one
way, and that is by contemplating Him.
He must be the Mirror which we consult,
and the Light by which we see. We must
look at His Beauty till we are changed into
His Likeness. We must consider His Perfection till we grow into it ourselves, not by
exterior imitation of Him, but by interior
union with Him. His sufferings will purify
us, His ministering will make us humble,
His meekness will teach us to obey, His
grace will make us modest, His truth will
be our light, His strength our endurance,
His love our all. Let the cross be signed
not only upon us, but within us, and we shall
find favour in His sight, and He will hold

out to us the golden sceptre that is in His hand, and receive us unto Himself.

We can behold Jesus everywhere, and become beautiful as we behold. It is love that beautifies. If we are bent on loving Him, nothing can possibly hinder us. We need not go into a convent in order to love Him. We will gladly go there if He will let us, but if He will not, then we will love Him where we are. We will shut our eyes to the world, and ask Him to manifest Himself to us. All the faculties of our being shall be directed to Him, we will not turn away one moment from looking upon Him. He will teach us wonderful things about Himself, and as we learn, He will enter into our soul, and take possession of it, and dwell there. Unconsciously we shall grow like Him; and some day—it will be the day of our heavenly nuptials—we shall wake up after His likeness, and shall be satisfied. May He be glorified in us for ever!

LETTER XII.

Of the Reward of Holy Virginity.

THE reward of all holiness is eternal life, —"this is life eternal, to know the only true God, and Jesus Christ." The reward of holy virginity, then, my sisters, is the same in kind as that of every other virtue. God can do what He will with His own, and He will give to the last as unto the first, to everyone eternal life, the knowledge of Himself.

Yet our Blessed Lord says, "In My Father's house are many mansions," meaning that though the happiness of all the elect is the same in kind, there are differences of degree. All will know God, and each will know Him to the utmost of his own capacity, but the capacities of souls vary almost infinitely, and some therefore will know Him more than others, that is, they will know Him in a higher degree. All will be satisfied, because all will be full, and souls in the lower mansions will not envy those in the higher mansions, because high and low alike will know all that they are capable of knowing, and all that God desires them to know.

He predestinated each soul for a special purpose, and in the fulfilment of that purpose the soul's eternal life, and its degree of divine knowledge consist. If all the elect were intended to know God in the same degree, there would be no meaning in distinct vocations, and no reason for individual character. Even on earth no two people apprehend a thing exactly in the same way, and so it will be in heaven. The eternal felicity of an infant who dies immediately after baptism, though identical in *kind*, will certainly differ in *degree* from that of a St. Paul, or a St. Athanasius. Those who have known most of God here will also know most of Him hereafter. The saint who from childhood has made God his study, who has given himself to the contemplation of divine things, and has all his life long conversed with angels rather than men, will undoubtedly enjoy a higher degree of divine knowledge in heaven, than the worldling who turns to God at the last moment, and dies making an act of perfect contrition. Both will be eternally happy, both will be perfectly happy, *i.e.* as happy as he can be, but one will be capable of a higher degree of happiness than the other.

The vocation to holy virginity is a call to know God, to know Him specially and intimately, with a knowledge transcending all other knowledge, the knowledge of espousals. To be joined to the Lord is to be made one spirit with Him, and the virgin is joined to Him in the highest degree of such mystical union. She puts from her all earthly joys that she may aspire to a heavenly alliance, and be made one spirit with Christ. Forsaking all other, she cleaves only to Him " Whom the angels lowly serve, Whose beauty sun and moon admire, Whose Mother is Ever-Virgin, and Who was begotten spiritually of His Father," and the result of this union with Him is to be an intimate, personal knowledge of Himself.

Unless we realize this, my sisters, we have no true sense of the dignity of our vocation. The virgin life is a life of divine knowledge; the Spirit that is given to us searcheth all things, yea, the deep things of God. " Eye hath not seen, nor ear heard, neither hath it entered man's heart, the things which God hath prepared for them that love Him. But God hath revealed them unto us by His Spirit." We have not got to wait for the revelation, it is ours already; it is the portion, even on earth, of the spouse of Christ.

The life of the virgin is a life of prayer, and by prayer the soul is illuminated, and made to understand all mysteries. Unless we are conscious within ourselves of this divine illumination, we have just reason to fear. Either we are not praying at all, or we are not praying enough, or we are not praying in the right way. We are called to know God, and He is only made known in prayer, by which is not here meant the offering up of petitions, but the steadfast interior gazing upon Him with the eye of the soul. "They had an eye unto Him, and were lightened," is the simple explanation of the wonderful knowledge of God which the saints have had. Divine things are spiritually discerned, they are foolishness to the natural heart. When we read of the knowledge which has come to many of God's servants in prayer, we are apt sometimes to think it a pious exaggeration: perhaps the reason of this is that we do not really ourselves know what it is to pray. Few people can believe in that of which they have no experience; if we had the saints' hatred of sin, we should better understand their love of prayer, and then the heavenly illuminations which they received from the Holy Ghost would not seem at all so incredible. I am not speaking of visions or ecstasies, which are not God's ordinary method, but only of those interior lights, which every soul may receive who prays with right dispositions, *i.e.* with a simple desire of knowing God, and of doing His Will.

"Blessed are the pure in heart, for they shall see God." The vision will be in proportion to the purity. The pure heart has no eyes but for God; in His light it sees light, and everything else is darkness. He is all its beauty, all its joy, all its desire; and out of Him and apart from Him it is blind, seeing nothing. All that is good honours God, and makes it rejoice. All that is evil dishonours Him, and makes it sorry. Here He is exalted, there He is disowned; but the pure heart sees Him everywhere, for good and evil both testify concerning Him that He is God. At all times and in all places the pure heart looks up, away from self, away from earth, and pierces the clouds, and enters heaven, and makes straight for God. If a work is to be undertaken it is done, not for the praise of men, nor even

M

chiefly for their benefit, but for the glory of God. If a sacrament is to be received, it is not merely in order to personal sanctification, but for the extension of His kingdom. If a vocation is granted, the pure heart rises up, and glorifies Him by its obedience. If a vocation is uncertain, it waits, and glorifies Him by its patience.

In sadness the pure heart sinks into the joy of God, and buries its sorrows there. In happiness it praises Him, and gives thanks for His great glory. It dwells under the defence of the most High, and abides under the shadow of the Almighty. Even in the midst of the world it can endure, "as seeing Him Who is invisible." Controversy does not disturb it, for it hides secretly in His tabernacle from the strife of tongues. Slander does not vex it, for it knows that God will plead its cause. It is not disheartened by failure, for He is its Reward; it does not fear danger, for He can preserve it. If it climbs up into heaven, God is there; if it goes down to hell, He is there also; if it takes the wings of the morning, and remains in the uttermost parts of the sea, even there also His hand shall lead it, and His right hand shall hold it. It is content with life, for to live is Christ. It will rejoice in death, for to die is gain.

If such is its present beatitude, what will be its future glory? If the virgin soul so lives and moves and has her being in God here, what will be her degree of union with God hereafter? St. John the Divine tells us, for it was specially revealed to him among the secrets of the kingdom of Heaven. "And I looked, and lo, a Lamb stood on the Mount Sion, and with Him an hundred forty and four thousand, having His Father's Name written in their foreheads. And I heard a voice from heaven, as the voice of many waters, and as the voice of a great thunder; and I heard the voice of harpers, harping with their harps, and singing as it were a new song before the throne, and before the four beasts and the elders; and no man could learn that song but the hundred and forty and four thousand which were redeemed from the earth. These are they which were not defiled with women, for they are virgins. These are they which follow the Lamb whithersoever He goeth; these were redeemed from among men, being the first-fruits unto God and to the Lamb. And in their mouth was found no guile; for they are without fault before the throne of God." (*Rev.* xiv.)

Four points may be noticed in this passage, as showing the special prerogatives of virgins, and the honour which is laid up for them in heaven. First, they will stand with the Lamb on the Mount; that is, that to them above others will be reserved the very highest place, the summit of the eternal glory. The Lamb is offered in sacrifice, slain from the foundation of the world, and they too have yielded themselves a living sacrifice to Him. He is without spot, they are without fault, and the union begun in suffering is perfected in glory; they will reign with Him in the highest for ever.

"Having His Father's Name written in their foreheads." Christ manifests His Father's Name to those whom God gives Him out of the world: "O righteous Father, the world hath not known Thee, but I have known Thee, and these have known that Thou hast sent Me. And I have declared unto them Thy Name, and will declare it; that the love wherewith Thou hast loved Me may be in them, and I in them." The Father begets the Son in love, and the very love wherein He begets Him is in them to whom

He is manifested. Virgins are redeemed from the earth with a redemption peculiarly their own, being the first-fruits unto God and to the Lamb. The Father's Name is written in their foreheads, and that Name is to them in a pre-eminent degree a revelation of divine love.

Another special glory of virgins is that they sing a new song that *no one but they can learn.* Others may listen to it perhaps, but only virgins will ever be able to sing it. It is a new song, a song that is, of the new covenant, the song of the Virgin-Born. It has to be learnt, and it is learnt through suffering. This thought should cheer us very much. The virginal sacrifice involves separation, loneliness; the spouse of Jesus, like her Lord, must tread the winepress alone. When the isolation is almost more than we can bear, let us remember this, my sisters: the new song which shall be ours, and which only the virgins can sing, must be learnt in loneliness. The separation, which is suffering here, will be glory hereafter.

" These are they which follow the Lamb whithersoever He goeth." This is the last, most glorious privilege of virgin-souls. To be with God in His high and holy place, and to be with Him for ever; to follow Him up to the heights of His glory, and down to the depths of His wisdom; to understand His justice, and partake of His mercy, and share in His goodness, and delight in His beauty; to reign with Him on His throne, and serve Him in His temple, and dwell with Him in His house for ever, with perfection of unitive love, the mutual love of the Bridegroom and the bride : this is the virgin's crown.

She whom the Lord hath betrothed to Himself with suffering, He will adorn as a bride with glory. He will clothe her with a garment of salvation, and cover her with a robe of gladness. He will call her by her name, saying, Thou art Mine. He will bid her draw near unto Him, and His Light shall shine upon her, and she will be like Him, for she will see Him as He is, in the splendour of His Godhead, and the beauty of His Manhood, Whose Name is Jesus.

This is the reward, dearest sisters, towards which we aspire. The virginal sacrifice is worth it, is it not? How is it that with such a glory before us we can ever be faint-hearted? The world and all its pomps we have despised for the love of Jesus Christ our Lord; already is His Flesh united to ours by the heavenly Food which He hath given us, and His Name is as ointment poured forth, therefore do we love Him. He knows that He has chosen us, and we, too, have chosen Him. To Him alone let us keep faith; to Him with full devotion let us give ourselves; and as we grow in purity, we shall also grow in that knowledge the fulness of which shall be our everlasting reward.

And in order that we may attain to this, let us ask our Lord to give us a great hatred of sin. Never let us speak or think lightly of the least venial sin; it will not cost us heaven, but it will delay our vision of God, and if we really love Him, will this be no cause for grief? Even our natural imperfections hinder our sight of Him, and must be mourned over, and corrected, and got rid of, before we can see Him. We must purify ourselves by penance if we hope to be illuminated in prayer, for a mote can hide the sunlight, and a sin can shut out God. The pure-hearted saint feels his need of penance far more than the newly-converted sinner, because he has a clearer knowledge of God, and has therefore learnt a truer estimate of sin. Our Immaculate Lord did supreme penance for sin, because, being God, He knew its utter hatefulness; and the soul that He espouses to Himself in virginal chastity will sink deeper in penance as it rises higher in purity. Then with the spirit of penance will come the spirit of prayer, and in the power of prayer we shall enter more and more into that light of knowledge which is the vision of God.

"Let Thy knowledge, O Lord, *here* grow in us, and in the world to come be full. Let Thy love grow *here*, and *there* be fulfilled; that *here* our joy may in hope be great, and *there* indeed find true consummation".* For this let our soul hunger, our flesh thirst after, our whole substance long for, till we are called to stand with Him in the heavenly Mount Sion, having His Father's Name written in our foreheads, and singing the new song which none can learn but they who follow the Lamb whithersoever He goeth. To Him be praise for ever!

* St. Anselm. "Prayers and Meditations."

LETTER XIII.
Of the Counsel of Evangelical Obedience.

JESUS be with you, sisters, and may His obedience perfect us in union with Himself. The life of evangelical perfection is a life of intimate union with God, through Jesus Christ our Lord. Its three Counsels of poverty, chastity, and obedience, include within themselves all the elements of that holiness which it is the object of the Incarnation to communicate to man, namely, the holiness of the most Blessed Trinity. The Word was made Flesh in order that flesh might be deified; He emptied Himself, that we might be filled. He offered Himself without spot to the Father, that we might be presented without spot unto Him, and He became obedient unto death, that we too, through obedience, might be made perfect. When, therefore, Christ speaks to a soul, and bids it follow Him in the way of Evangelical Perfection, and when the soul, answering to that call, rises up and follows, it pledges itself wholly and without reserve to the fulfilment, not of one or other, but of all the Gospel Counsels. We, then, my sisters, to whom this call is given, must be not only entirely poor, and entirely chaste, but entirely obedient too; otherwise we shall never fulfil our vocation, which is to be like Christ, nor attain to the end of our being, which is union with God. Holy poverty leads us through the purgative way, cleansing our hearts from all attachment to creatures, and emptying it of all unworthy objects; and holy chastity introduces us into the illuminative way, and inflames our love and desire by showing us the beauty of God; but holy obedience lifts us up into the unitive way, and fulfils our desire, binding us irrevocably to Him in the union of Divine love itself.

Let us, again, remind ourselves that in observing the Evangelical Counsels it is the perfection of Jesus at which we aim, and by means of which we are to be perfected. Just as we take Him for our model of poverty, and learn of Him how to empty ourselves; just as He teaches us in chastity how to purify ourselves as He is pure, so too must we go to Him to be made obedient by the things which we shall suffer. He is the living book which we must always be studying; and though we may read of heroic obedience in the lives of saints, just as we read of their unearthly purity and absolute poverty, yet after all it is Jesus, and Jesus only Who can conquer us, and enter in, and take possession of us, and make us divine. And this is what we want, this is the only true meaning of perfection, this is why we have stripped ourselves of possessions and affections and will, that He may dwell in us and we in Him, in a unity like that of the Manhood with the Godhead, and of the Blessed Trinity of Persons in the Divine Unity of Substance.

We must be obedient, then, with the obedience of Jesus, just as we are to be poor with His poverty, and chaste with His chastity. By obedience is meant subjection to the will of another; by evangelical obedience, subjection to God as supreme, and to man as the representative of God; and by religious obedience, subjection under God to superiors appointed or sanctioned by ecclesiastical authority. All men are called upon to practise in some degree obedience of the first kind, which is not necessarily a virtue; many Christians are counselled to follow Christ in evangelical obedience, which is a divine virtue; and some are further called to practise also religious obedience, which is a virtue peculiar to the religious state. In this letter we will think only of that evangelical obedience which is necessary to perfection.

St. Paul, in speaking of the Incarnation, says, "God *sent* forth His Son, made of a woman" (*Gal.* iv. 4), and our Lord's whole Incarnate life is a divine mission, *i.e.* a sending. This at once brings before us the fact of His obedience, not as a mere occasional virtue, nor as a feature appearing from time to time, and giving a look of additional humility to some of His actions, but as the general characteristic of His whole human life, the attitude which He maintains in His created nature, His position as Man towards God. To a thoughtful mind it means more than this, and indicates the relation of the Eternal Son to the Eternal Father; but for the present we will not dwell upon this thought. It will be enough to consider the obedience of Christ as revealed to us in the Gospel narrative.

It is important to remember that our Lord's obedience, like His poverty, was both actual and voluntary. He did willingly all that He had to do. He yielded absolute obedience to God, and relative obedience to man, for God's sake; He fulfilled the law to the letter, and He fulfilled it in the spirit also. Everything that He ever did, from the first moment of His Incarnation till He gave up the ghost on Calvary, was an act of obedience. When He came into the world, He said, "I come to do Thy Will, O God," and, though it cost Him His life, He was content to do it; His Father's law was within His Heart, and He nourished Himself by it, and made obedience to be His very meat. "My meat," He said, "is to do the Will of Him that sent Me;" and every word that proceedeth out of the Mouth of God was bread unto Him. He declared Himself only able to do those things which He saw the Father do : the works that He did were the works of the Father, the words that He uttered were the words of the Father, and the doctrine that He taught was the doctrine He had received of the Father. His attitude towards God was a creaturely attitude; He looked to Him to be taught, both how to speak, and what to do. The world was to be redeemed by the Son, but it was to be redeemed in the Father's way, often at a cost to the Son's pure Human Nature. "He must be about His Father's business," though it sent a sword through His Mother's soul, and He drank the cup of sorrow to the dregs, though it cost Him an agony and sweat of blood. "Not My will, but Thine," was the motto of the whole Incarnate Life of God, just as it must be the motto of every human life that aspires to be divine. "I have finished the work which Thou gavest Me to do," is the epitomized history of Christ in His Incarnation; and so in its degree it must be the summary of the life of every saint.

Taught by Christ, the obedient soul looks to God as the Father, Whose perfect way must be followed, Whose words of truth must be spoken, and Whose works of righteousness must be fulfilled. It readily keeps His Commandments, and, not content with these, it follows His Counsels too. It fears no danger but that of independence, and shrinks from no venture that it is called to make for God's sake and in union with Him. It is always contented, for it knows the certainty of His Providence, and always triumphant, for man's failure is God's victory! Obedience shines brightest in dark times, and in long watches, for then it looks most steadily to God, and unconsciously catches His light. It learns its first lessons from Christ, the First-Born of every creature, and studies as divine revelations of Him the order of His manifold operations in the triple creation of nature, grace, and glory ; it sees angels and men and brute beasts, visible weakness and invisible force, growth and decay and resurrection, consciously or unconsciously gathered round the Father's Throne "in order serviceable;" it recognises that obedience is the creature's sole prerogative and highest blessedness, and it thanks God that He is God, and that all things serve Him. Obedience is heaven begun already, for what is the creature's heaven but this—absolute dependence upon God, and union with Him by perfect service ?

That man should obey God ought to be no great wonder, for he was made for no other purpose ; but the Gospel goes beyond this, and shows us God yielding obedience to man, for God's sake. It shows us the Creator willingly allowing Himself to be enrolled as His own creature's subject. It shows Him placing Himself at the mercy of selfish Bethlehemites, who refused His Mother a shelter and Him a place to be born in. He obeyed not Cæsar only, but the innkeeper too, for He came to Bethlehem at the order of the one, and went to the stable in obedience to the other. His flight into Egypt was an act of obedience to human authority, for it seemed to recognize Herod's right to murder the Innocents if he chose, and it looked as if flight were the only means by which He could save Himself. He Who had led Israel out of Egypt suffered Himself to be carried back to it by His fugitive parents; and when His exile was over He yielded submission to their fear, and allowed them to take Him to the ill-famed Nazareth rather than to the city of David. There He was subject to them as a Child, Who was very and Eternal God. He, the divine Wisdom, consented to be taught by His creatures; He obeyed their wishes, and carried out their instructions. He toiled in a workshop, and earned bread in the sweat of His brow, He, the Living Bread, that came down from heaven! In the Temple, during the three days' loss, He listened to the doctors, and asked them questions, though all the treasures of divine knowledge lay hid in Him. Again, at His parents' wish He came down to

Nazareth, and was subject unto them, and for eighteen years, though divinely occupied no doubt, with the sanctification of His blessed Mother, He was humanly under obedience to her, with no other visible avocation than that of a village carpenter.

When His ministry began, His sphere of obedience widened. He placed Himself at the disposal of all who needed Him. "What wilt thou that I should do for thee?" was His question to those who came to Him in distress. Virtue went out from Him at the mere touch of faith. Whatever faith desired of Him that He did, with an obedience that was human, though the power it wielded was divine. He would pay tribute to Cæsar, and answer questions of the Sadducees, and eat with publicans and sinners. In all things not contrary to the will of God He obeyed the will of man, and He obeyed it readily, not counting the cost to Himself. His days were so taken up with serving men, that sometimes He had not leisure so much as to eat, and He had to reserve the nights for lonely communings with God. Even these were not always uninterrupted, for once He left His prayers to go to His disciples who were toiling on a stormy sea, though He might have brought them to land in a moment without going to them had He willed; so true it was of Him, in life as well as in death, that Himself He would not save. Whenever He acted otherwise, and used His own authority, as when He drove the changers out of the Temple, or looked with anger upon those that were round about, or sent a stern message to Herod, it was because His Father's honour was at stake, or because His Father's commandment was broken; never to avenge a personal wrong to Himself, nor to secure to Himself a personal right.

But the obedience of the Creator to His creatures is chiefly shown in the Passion. For then Divine Love suffered the kiss that He knew meant betrayal, and Omnipotence gave Himself up into the hands of weakness, and allowed Himself to be bound with cords, and led away to prison. Uncreated Light submitted to be blindfolded, and Uncreated Beauty was smitten on the face. God was charged with blasphemy; the Lord of all stood before governors and rulers; Omniscience was arrayed in a fool's garment; the King of kings was crowned with thorns; Eternal Truth was spit upon; Divine Mercy was scourged; Righteousness was numbered with the transgressors; Life was condemned to death : and all this with the willing consent of a perfectly free obedience. "No man," He said, "taketh My life from Me : I lay it down of Myself." This was a work He had seen of the Father; a secret He had learnt in the Bosom of God, where from all eternity He had beheld Himself, in the divine predestination "the Lamb slain from the foundation of the world." Let us always remember (for it is a gospel in itself) that it was the obedience of Christ, not His mere suffering, the spirit of the Passion rather than the Passion itself, that glorified God and saved the world.

Jesus Christ is the same, yesterday and to-day and for ever. The obedience of His human Life on earth is perpetuated in the mystery of the Blessed Sacrament. He comes to us or He stays away, according to our will. He could claim to be uplifted every day on every altar of Christendom, yet He does not assert His right to the daily Mass. "His delights are to be with the sons of men," and, if only we believed in prayer, we could pray Him back to our midst, to abide with us in His tabernacles for ever. But we are not ready for Him yet; we do not desire Him. It is obedience that keeps Jesus away from us, a most merciful obedience; for what would not our guilt be if, with the reserved Sacrament in our churches, we were to continue what we are? He is always being told that He is not wanted here in England, at least not in sacramental ways, which are His chosen, special ways, the ways He loves, and has blessed. He will not come to us unless we will; so far His will and ours are one. In what overwhelming responsibilities does not this involve us? For in a true but undefinable sense, is not every communion an act of obedience on our Lord's part? and think what our bad communions have cost Him. We wonder at the obedience of Bethlehem, but our bad communions have demanded from Him a harder obedience than that, for surely they were among the supreme sorrows of His Calvary. He might withdraw from the Sacred Host if He willed; He has the power to do so, just as He had power to save Himself, and come down from the Cross; but rather than exercise His Omnipotence thus, He makes Himself obedient still, and submits to the indignities of our bad communions, because, in some mysterious way, a glory is thus secured to God that would otherwise be lost. The obedience of the Passion and of the Blessed Sacrament is one and the same. It brings out in high relief the submission of the whole Incarnate Life, and sets before us the standard at which we are to aim, and the only one with which we can ever be content. Nothing short of this is that obedience of the Gospel which Evangelical Perfection demands.

We must pray, then, dearest sisters, to be filled with the obedience of Jesus. We cannot imitate it, we must *have* it: and, believe me, there is no better school of obedience than one's own secular home. There we have abundant opportunity of perpetually submitting ourselves to others, for parents have a right to demand our submission as long as they live, in all things not affecting our direct duty to God; and elders will never cease to treat us as children, and youth will claim our services whenever they are required, and will ignore us when they are not. If there are no rules to keep there will be whims to respect; and who are more exacting of obedience than whimsical people? It not unfrequently happens in the world that a person of full age and of apparent independence is in actual, though secret, subjection to others. The yoke is no easy one, but, though galling, it is not dishonourable; and, if well borne, it will be very sanctifying. Human nature finds it hard to be "without honour in one's own house," yet that is a common experience with those who are called to perfection in the world. Swaddling clothes are irksome when one feels the full vigour of the prime of life. Years ago we looked forward to our independence, but it has not come yet; we begin to suspect that it never will. We might, of course, assert it, but that would be against the spirit of our vocation. We are growing grey, perhaps, yet we cannot give an order in our own home, nor express an opinion freely. We should think that we are getting into our second childhood, only we are quite aware that we have never outgrown our first. And then we have spiritual books, and our religious friends, gravely assuring us that "obedience" is impossible for seculars! We smile, and venture to think that, for once, spiritual books and religious are slightly mistaken. At least, they assure us, the obedience of seculars is not so meritorious as religious obedience, and this point we will not contest. We

OF EVANGELICAL OBEDIENCE. 183

must leave the question of merit to those whom it concerns, and apply ourselves with all our might to cultivate the grace which lies within our reach. Evangelical obedience, which is that of Christ Himself, shall suffice to us; and if we try in all things to obey as He obeyed, although we may not "merit" much, He will love us none the less.

Let us ask·Him, then, to enter into our heart, and subdue it in obedience unto Himself. If we ask Him in faith He will take us at our word, and that blessed day will be to us as heaven begun on earth. For then the Father's will shall be our meat, and His work our joy. We shall speak truth, and know doctrine, and be one with God and He with us. Then, too, we shall obey man, and every ordinance of man, for God's sake. We shall submit ourselves not only to the good and gentle, but also to the froward; we shall not speak evil of dignities, but shall yield ourselves in silence to their decrees; and if at times (as will surely be the case) obedience is hard, and nature rises against what seems unjust, or false, or cruel, one look at our crucifix, one aspiration to Jesus in His Blessed Sacrament, will suffice to bring us to a better mind: for the worst that man can do is to crucify us, and that, if only we are willing, shall secure us in eternal union with the Lord Whom we love. May He be glorified in us for ever!

LETTER XIV.

Of Spiritual Direction.

THE way of perfection, my sisters, is one in which no soul can safely walk alone. It is beset on all sides with dangers, and every turn of the road presents new difficulties, which will soon dishearten the timid, and prove a snare to the brave, if they attempt to direct themselves. Holy Scripture says, "Woe to him that is alone when he falleth, for he hath not another to help him up" (*Eccl.* iv.); and those who aim at perfection must be prepared for many failures, which, however, are not likely to prove irremediable so long as they are under the direction of a spiritual guide, but which may any time be fatal if they are not. "Lean not unto thine own understanding, and be not wise in thine own eyes." (*Prov.* iii.)

The soul that tries to guide itself in the way of perfection will most infallibly fail of its end, and will probably lose itself altogether.

The example of the saints sufficiently proves the necessity of spiritual direction, for none of them, however advanced they might be in the paths of virtue, ever dreamt of directing themselves. They knew that the kingdom of heaven must be received in the spirit of little children, that is, with docility and obedience. Without this no growth in perfection is possible, for the perfect life is one of submission, and the natural spirit of man inclines to independence; the perfect life is humble and hidden, and the natural spirit delights in vain show and importance; the perfect life is one of self-renunciation, and the natural spirit tends to sensuality and carnal pleasures. Besides which, the soul needs to be instructed both what to fight against, and how to fight; sometimes it needs encouragement, and sometimes rebuke; it must know how to defend itself against the wiles of the devil, how to overcome the weakness of the flesh, how to disdain the allurements of the world, and how to triumph over the opposition of friends and family, "the foes of a man's own household," against which our Blessed Lord especially warns those whom He calls to perfection.

The soul that enters this way is exposed also to every kind of spiritual danger, such, for example, as illusions, which are often presented to it under the appearance of good, the evil one being able to transform himself into an angel of light; or the indiscreet practice of bodily austerities (an exceedingly rare danger in these days, but a very real one where it exists); or a selfish love of solitude; or lengthened and multiplied devotions; or extraordinary methods of prayer, or mistaken practices of virtue—*e.g.* a too ardent zeal, a too apparent humility, or an indolent sweetness of temper. In all such matters the soul is incapable of judging for itself, and needs the counsel of an experienced guide; as also in considering those interior operations which may be most precious and heavenly inspirations on the one hand, or, on the other, most sad, and even fatal, illusions.

Again, certain conditions to which the spiritual life is subject require not only a guide, but a physician too. By this is not here meant actual sins, which must be got rid of in confession, and for the healing of which a special sacrament and ministry have been instituted by our Lord Himself. The remedy for sin is Penance, but the remedy for certain states of the soul which, though not in themselves sinful, tend to sin, is direction.

Discouragement after a humiliating fall is not at all an uncommon thing, but unless remedied by a skilful director it will lead to despair. Interior dryness, during which the soul finds itself unable to speak to God freely, or even to think of Him with joy, is a condition which calls for the help and consolation of a good director; while it certainly needs a stronger hand and will than their own to shake souls out of the lukewarmness into which, when their first fervours are over, so many relapse, and which is the cause of perdition to not a few.

But the persons who most of all need spiritual direction are the scrupulous. "A scrupulous man" has been well described as one who "teases God, irritates his neighbour, torments himself, and oppresses his director;"* and a scruple is defined in theology to be "a vain fear of sin where there is

* Faber: "Growth in Holiness," ch. xvii.

no reason, nor reasonable ground, for suspecting sin." Scruples are quite distinct from delicacy of conscience, which is known by its not only being reasonable, but, much more, by its being tranquil. They arise from different causes, the commonest of which are perhaps an excessive fear of God's justice, or a distrust of His mercy. But whatever may be the cause of them, the remedy is always the same, and that is blind and absolute obedience to a spiritual guide. The scrupulous person has a diseased conscience, and in order that it may be cured he must be willing to act upon the conscience of another, and the chief sin which such an one should stand in fear of is disobedience, for unless he obeys he will certainly fall into many sins, which by obedience he will as certainly avoid.

A director, then, is necessary, in order to teach us what we ought to know, what we ought to avoid, and what we ought to practise. It is quite true that we can find out many of these things in books, but books sometimes do as much harm as good, because we have no means at all of knowing what we ought to apply to ourselves; and it is certain that what may be very good medicine for one would be poison to another. We cannot trust to our own discrimination in such matters, and we need some one else to tell us not only what is good in itself, but—which is of far more importance—what is good for us. And since every soul is either a traveller who needs a guide, or an invalid who needs a doctor, or a convalescent who needs a support, or an apprentice who needs a master, it is clear that direction, which supplies to each soul the kind of help that it needs, is necessary for all, and that, not only at certain periods of life, at the beginning of spiritual conversion, or in times of special danger, but always and in all circumstances. The soul that submits to direction is free and walks at liberty, for it is never in doubt about its action, which is ruled not according to self-will, but by obedience.

The necessity of a director, the account which we must give to him of ourselves, and the docility with which we should allow him to guide us, is a subject which flesh and blood revolts from, which human prudence cannot understand, and which the wise of this world will not submit to Yet the Fathers of the Church have believed it to be of such importance that they have taught it as the very alphabet of the spiritual life, as a fundamental of the Christian religion, and as a necessary principle for all who would learn the Gospel of Jesus Christ.

Having seen the necessity of spiritual direction, let us now go on to consider its advantages, first as it affects the general life of a religious community, and then its effect upon the individual soul. The holiness of a community consists in the union of its members among themselves, and in their unity of aim and purpose. This union and this unity cannot possibly exist among a number of persons, all with different temperaments and characters, unless they are trained so to modify their individual tastes that they come to have a way of seeing and doing things common to the community as a whole ; and this can only be effected by means of direction, and of one method of direction for all. The director will know the individual character of each religious, and will be able to train each so that she may adapt herself to the general rule, and to her own relations towards her sisters. He will thus form souls in the spirit of their society, and will produce among them that divine attraction which is essential to the happiness of a community.

They will be formed in virtue, and established in religion, and they will be drawn to God by the interior spirit of faith and of prayer. There must also be the same direction for all, if the peace of the community is to be preserved. Good direction removes bitterness, prevents party spirit, and secures a general sweetness, strength, and healthiness of tone which nothing else can give.

The advantages to the individual are also very apparent. There are times when we feel that we can no longer keep ourselves to ourselves. We must speak to someone—our hearts are full, and they must overflow. Unless we can find spiritual relief we shall turn to natural succours, and that in a religious, or indeed in any soul with a vocation to perfection, is a serious defect, if not actually a sin; or else, if we are proof against this weakness, we shall only fall into some other, and give way to sadness, or even perhaps to laxity or sensuality. The safeguard against this lies in spiritual direction; it will not only relieve the heart, it will enlarge it also; it will give us holy liberty, and secure for us a wise friend, who, if he reproves us, will cheer us too, and who will keep us at peace with ourselves and with God, Whom we are certain to please so long as we obey our director. True, he is not himself infallible. With the best of intentions he may make mistakes, and may err in directing us; but *we* cannot err so long as we obey him, for God will overrule his error, and will bless our obedience, and perfect that which is imperfect both in him and in us. Direction helps us to advance in virtue, shows us our weak points, and suggests methods of improvement; it throws new light upon our path, and cheers us on to persevere. It also ensures us the happiness of holy friendship, for direction brings into contact not only heart with heart, but soul with soul—that is to say, the friendship is not one of mere affection, but of innermost being. The director sees not only the good in a soul, but the evil also, and he cares for it notwithstanding. The soul, too, recognizes in its director not a human friend who will flatter it, but a spiritual friend, who is bound for God's sake to be true to it, and to tell it not the best about itself—or, if the best, the worst also. The soul that thus yields obedience to spiritual direction lives in peace, walks in freedom, grows in humility and every virtue, keeps steadfast to its resolutions, and abounds in consolation. The soul that scorns direction is blinded by pride, beset by fears, lives in bondage, makes no advance in virtue, is inconstant, wavering, and scrupulous. This is the best that can be said of it, and the only thing that makes its condition not altogether hopeless is that its very misery will perhaps drive it some day to seek a spiritual guide. But if it is not conscious of misery its case is almost hopeless, for it is walking headlong to perdition.

The director may be either the confessor or some other priest; or, in a community of men, the superior, who may be a layman; or, in a community of women, the mother superior. Spiritual direction is a necessary part of the religious life, by which I mean that there is no choice whatever about it; it is part of the rule which has to be observed. Religious cannot choose their director, as seculars may, and many find it a most trying ordeal to be obliged to open their souls to a person to whom perhaps they have no attraction whatever, and for whom they may possibly even feel some repugnance. Under such circumstances a religious might be dispensed for a time from direction, which is only of use when confidence is freely given

o

and received; but for the sake of the community, which would suffer if this were allowed to go on, the religious would try to overcome her aversion, and to submit to direction like the rest. To go to direction in the spirit of perfect obedience, doing one's best to fulfil a disagreeable duty as well as possible, would be an almost heroic action in the sight of God, Who would certainly reward it with abundant grace. For what pleases Him in the matter is, neither the holiness of the director, nor the confidence given him, but the docility with which the soul yields itself to be directed; and if we are put under a director whom we ourselves would not have chosen, let us be content with the thought that he is God's choice for us, and that he has all the grace necessary for our present sanctification. After all, it is God Who has charge of our souls, and He can and will give us always just the director whom He knows to be best for us. If only we are simple, no director will be allowed to hinder us in the way of perfection; if he is stern, he will be as a schoolmaster to bring us to Christ, and if he is cold and hard he will drive us home all the closer to our Heavenly Father's breast. I believe that when God allows a soul to suffer from its director it is only that He may draw it into a deeper union with Himself; and unless at some time or other the soul does so suffer, it misses a means of sanctification which cannot be so well effected in any other way.

What has just been said applies chiefly, though not altogether, to religious, seculars being for the most part free in their choice of a director. Generally, too, for persons living in the world the confessor and the director should be one. Where this can be done it avoids complications, and ensures a better understanding; but, of course, there are exceptions to this rule as to every other. Any authorized priest can hear a confession, but not all confessors are good directors, and if we have the choice of a director we are bound to choose the best we can; the best, that is, for our soul's needs, not the one whom we personally admire, or feel attracted to, and certainly not the one whom we think will flatter or indulge us. The good director is a man of piety, learning, and experience, his duty being to perfect and adorn the soul for God. He must not be a man of prejudices, but of sober good sense, large-minded certainly, and, if possible, large-hearted, too.

The choice of a director is one of the most serious responsibilities that ever comes to us in life, and that soul is happy whom circumstances and the kind providence of God have saved from having to make it. It should never be settled in a hurry, the only safety at such times being in prayer and much patience. "God, Who sees the heart, will reward us according to our faith. Let our only object in seeking a director be that we may altogether die to ourselves and to our own will; and then God, Who never fails the true-hearted, will give us the guide whom we desire, as He sent the angel Raphael to Tobit. Only let us be humble, and detached from all self-interest, and let us become as little children, and the director whom we seek will be surely given to us."*

Having found a director let us keep to him, and not be always on the look-out to get direction from half-a-dozen others. Love of change is fatal to the spiritual life, and so is all unnecessary talk about ourselves. But while we are careful on the one hand not to have a number of directors, we must not on the other hand cling too tenaciously to one. It is sometimes necessary to change our direc-

* St. Francis of Sales.

tor, and it is almost a sure sign that we ought to do so if we cease to feel at ease with him. There must be no bondage in direction, though there must often be not only absolute, but also blind, obedience. When our relation with our director ceases to be of a perfectly filial nature, it is time that it came to an end, for in that case his direction will be doing us only harm. We must be careful not to allow ourselves in any undue attachment to him, and we may recognise by the following signs if our attachment goes beyond what is allowable :—

1. We shall wish for his esteem. 2. Under cover of humility we shall draw his attention to our supposed good qualities. 3. We shall allow him to know that we think him indispensable to our perfection. 4. We shall be jealous of the time and thought he bestows upon others. 5. We shall be endless in our interviews with him. 6. Uneasy at an occasional absence. 7. Over-anxious with respect to his health. 8. Unwilling, if he is also our confessor, to make our confessions to any other priest. 9. Careful to assist, and even to communicate, at his masses, in preference to those of other priests; and of all the follies in which any one can indulge, this is per-

haps the most contemptible and the most profane.

The soul, then, that would profit by direction must be perfectly simple. It will pray for the director, and so give him the only reward that he desires. It will be docile, never asking reasons for anything, but obeying at once and without reserve; it will also be humble, being quite as ready to accept reproof as consolation, not greedy of comfort, but grateful to know the truth about itself.

Certain things clearly furnish matter for direction, while some are indifferent, and others altogether irrelevant. Some souls need more minute direction than others. It would be easy to say that discretion will guide us in seeking direction; but, unhappily, discretion is a very rare grace. Let us make a rule, then, of only asking direction in such matters as we should speak to our Lord about, if He were personally Himself our director. We should not take up His time with the foolish trivialities which too many love to get themselves directed about. If only we would follow that simple Apostolic rule, of doing *everything* "as to the Lord," how easy it would all become! Why is it that our life is the dull lesson we so often find it, but because we are always perversely going out of God's sunshine into the shade of our own self-consciousness ?

Let us ask to be directed what virtues to acquire, and how to acquire them ; how to overcome temptation, and how to act both in defeat and victory. Let us set ourselves, under direction, to discipline not our soul and mind only, but our body also ; and let us hand ourselves over to be formed for God's own uses. For this reason our desires and aspirations should be made known to the director, for unless we tell him of these he can have only a partial knowledge of us. As to vocation and work, the only happiness for us is to submit to his judgment. It is not likely that he will make a mistake, but, if he does, God can rectify it. Souls are sometimes trained for their real work by being put to do things they were never meant for ; and if it only makes them die to self, they are doing the most splendid work of all, without the disadvantage of its being apparent. Some hungry souls are always spreading banquets for others, which they are never to feast upon themselves ; some, like signposts in a wilderness, are always pointing the way to fair regions which they themselves shall never attain to; while others are perpetually working the treadmill of disappointment; some are told that the vocation they seem to hear so plainly, is not a vocation at all; others are kept in suspense for years; one soul is sent almost at once into religion, while another is detained in the world. This is what comes of spiritual direction; and to put oneself under a director is to subject oneself to such possibilities. Painful no doubt, but most salutary; for it ensures not to religious only, but to souls living in the world in a nominal independence, the grace of being in subjection to the will of another; and that, believe me, is one of the most blessed of all graces. Without it we cannot attain to perfection, but with it, under God, the highest sanctity becomes possible to us; for with the oblation of our own free will we yield ourselves living sacrifices unto Him, and our eternal predestination to His glory is most safely and most certainly fulfilled. May He be praised above all for ever!

LETTER XV.

Of Religious Obedience.

FOR those of us, my sisters, who may be awaiting our call to the religious state, it is important that something should here be said on the subject of religious obedience; and as this is a matter which is generally but little understood, and one which is open to great misconception, I shall not trust myself to speak to you in my own words. This letter will therefore contain hardly anything that is original, and if it seems to you drier than some of the others, it will really be far more worth your attention, for I shall be speaking to you almost in the words of that great master of the religious life, St. Ignatius Loyola. It is from a letter addressed by him on this subject to the religious of his own order, that most of what follows is taken.

The religious is bound to obey the superior, and, as will be explained in another letter, any breach of religious obedience is not only a moral and spiritual, but also an ecclesiastical offence. To worldly-minded persons this looks like tyranny, but any thoughtful Christian will see at once that, if undertaken in the true evangelical spirit, there is no liberty to be compared with that which is secured by the religious vow of obedience. It simplifies the entire life, and reduces perfection to a single practice, for he who obeys perfectly does all things well. Moreover, a canonically-appointed superior, by the very terms of appointment, does not rule arbitrarily and absolutely, nor would any command that might be given contrary to the law of God be of weight, nor, in such a case, ought the religious to obey. God is always to be obeyed rather than man, and the superior is to be obeyed as acting for God, which could not be if an immoral command were given. The tyranny of the religious state, if such tyranny exists, is due to some fault in the individual, and not to any in the state. Compared with the tyranny of the world it is freedom indeed, for religion is order, and order implies harmony, and harmony is regulated freedom. It is precisely the lack of this regulated freedom that makes life in the world to be the tyranny it is. Independence is not freedom; order is freedom, and in order there necessarily exists dependence, that is, of the inferior upon the superior. The spirit of the world is essentially disorderly, and the Christian loves divine order, and is always striving after it. It exists perfectly in heaven, but nowhere at all on earth, except in the Catholic church, and in the religious state.

The soul that aspires to perfection in the world will soon find this out. Technically, religious obedience is not possible to the secular, yet something not altogether unlike it is possible, though very hard. Everyone who wishes to be perfect must of course live according to rule ; some definite rule, affecting both the interior and exterior conduct. This rule would be drawn up under direction, and a sacred promise might be made, of obedience to the director, and fidelity to the rule. In all matters not affecting this rule, and not contrary to the counsel of the director nor to the law of God, unlimited obedience might be given to all persons whatsoever. Let a soul living in the world give itself to practise obedience on this principle, and, if less technical than the obedience of the religious state, it will not on that account be easier. The religious obeys her canonical superiors, those who have a right to command her, and whom she has vowed to obey; but the secular acting thus has to yield obedience to everyone, without the protection of authority or the support of a vow. The religious at least will never be blamed for her obedience; but the secular will always be getting into trouble for it. Obedience to her director and to her rule of life, the causes of which are invisible to the world, will get called self-will, while her compliance with the wishes of others, no matter what it may cost her, will often be attributed to indolence or folly. This is the world's estimate; God, who reads the heart, judges very differently.

But to return to the subject of religious obedience in its stricter sense.

The motive which prompts to religious obedience is supplied by the fact that the superior represents to the community our Lord Jesus Christ Himself. In obeying the superior a religious obeys God, and as God demands an entire obedience on man's part, it follows that the religious must yield an entire obedience to the superior.

There are three degrees in obedience. The first is *execution*, which means the outward fulfilment of the command, obedience in the letter. This doing what one is told to do is quite essential to obedience, which could not exist without it, but it does not in itself constitute the virtue of obedience. It must also be accompanied by *union of will*. This second degree makes the will of the inferior one with that of the superior, and makes them agree so well together, that not only that thing is done which was commanded, but it is so done as to show that the will and intention of both are the same, and that they each will, or do not will, the same things. This is what Holy Scripture means when it says, To obey is better than sacrifice; for victims offered in sacrifice are not one's own flesh, but obedience sacrifices one's own will. And because the will is the noblest of all man's faculties, therefore the sacrifice of it is especially pleasing to God.

This obedience must be universal, and must be observed not only in things relating to the exterior life, but in those also that affect the interior. It is as truly a breach of obedience to go beyond the rule in such matters as mortification, fasting, and prayer, as it is to fall short of it, or to indulge secretly in personal vanity, or open neglect of duty. The business of Martha and the contemplation of Mary were both holy, but what made them so is the fact that they were done in Bethany, by which is to be understood, mystically, "the house of obedience," which the word Bethany means. So we see that neither the desire for good works, nor the love of holy contemplation, are really acceptable to our Lord unless they are done in obedience.

This submission of the will sacrifices to God the liberty which He Himself has given, and it is surely no small thing to be able by such an act to make Him altogether supreme in the soul. Far from losing one's liberty, this sacrifice secures and perfects it; for the will is thus always conformed to that of God, as it should be faithfully interpreted by the commands of the superior, appointed in His Name by His Church's authority. For this reason religious should never try, either directly or indirectly, to influence the will of the superior, for that would not be to conform their will to the will of God, but rather to accommodate the divine will to their own, thus upsetting the whole order of God's wisdom concerning them.

The second degree of obedience must, therefore, lead on to the third, which is *sub-*

mission of judgment. Now, though the judgment is not free in its operations, which the will is, and inclines naturally to that which it judges to be best, yet, where things appear to be of equal merit, it may incline to one or to another, according to the dictates of the will. In all matters of indifference, then, the religious should share the judgment of the superior, because obedience is a kind of burnt-offering, in which the whole life is sacrificed in the flames of divine love by the hands of God's ministers. It is also a perfect renunciation of self, by which the religious willingly resigns all right to regulate her individual actions, in order to depend absolutely upon the providence of God in submission to her superior; so that obedience does not consist only in the execution of things commanded, nor in the willingness with which they are done, but also in submission of the judgment by which, so far as possible, the inferior approves of everything which is commanded by the superior.

This obedience of the judgment is quite indispensable to all who would live well in religion. As in the heavenly bodies the action of each is regulated by its relative position towards the others, so also among the members of a community. In order that they may work together under authority, those who submit themselves to the *will* of the superior, must also be subject to the *discretion* of the superior, which is not possible unless the will and the judgment are both completely surrendered.

The will is not proof against self-interest, and neither is the judgment. If in worldly affairs no one trusts entirely to himself, but seeks the advice of another in order to defer to his judgment, there should be no great difficulty in yielding oneself to a religious superior who represents God to the soul. The devil is well pleased if he can get a religious first to neglect counsel, and then to rest in her own judgment, and to follow her own lights; because he knows that in so doing she will almost certainly be lost. Where there is no submission of judgment, or only an imperfect submission, the will itself cannot be entirely submitted, and even the execution of the things ordered to be done, and which in a manner are done, will be defective. Those only obey well who obey cheerfully—that is, with promptness, joy, and zeal. Nothing is difficult to the humble soul, and nothing irritates the meek.

Only let us yield ourselves to God in meekness and humility, and He will give us grace gladly to fulfil the vows by which we have bound ourselves to His service.

Three considerations may be helpful in acquiring submission of the judgment. The first is, to regard the superior not as subject to ordinary defects and failings, but as representing Christ, the Wisdom of God, Whose goodness is supreme, and Whose love is infinite, and Who can neither deceive nor be deceived. Bearing this in mind it will be easy to obey, for though we may not understand the reason of what we are commanded, and though it may, in itself, appear to be foolish, yet if done "as to the Lord," and not to men, it will certainly be of great benefit to the soul, and we shall be able by means of it to glorify God to an extent which would not be possible if we fully understood the reason for the command.

Secondly, we must always do all that we can, to justify to ourselves and to others the orders of the superiors, and never allow ourselves to express disapproval of *any command whatsoever*, provided that it is not contrary to the law of God. We must try as far as possible not only to do, but to will, and to love, that which is commanded, and then our obedience will be free indeed.

Thirdly, we must be thoroughly convinced that every command of the superior is in fact a command of God Himself, and just as we accept in faith all that the Church proposes to us to be believed, so we should yield ourselves in blind obedience to do all that the superior tells us, without question and without reserve. If it should happen that we doubt the lawfulness of any command (if we *know* it to be unlawful we shall not be in doubt), we may mention our doubt to the superior, but it must be with a perfectly ready will to abide absolutely by her ultimate decision, which we shall accept as the voice of God.

This brief summary of the teaching of St. Ignatius will perhaps suffice to shew us all that we need at present understand of the principle of religious obedience. It is an easy yoke compared with that which the world would make us wear, and which, so long as we remain in the secular state, it is always trying to force upon us. Some day, perhaps, our Lord will call us aside from the multitude, and will place upon our neck the yoke that we long for; and for those of us whom He shall so call what a happy day that will be! For then He will bind us to Himself, irrevocably and for ever, with the cords of an obedience that shall not be perfectly evangelical only, but perfectly religious too. May He grant this to us whom He has taught to desire it, and so shall His Will and ours be completely fulfilled. To Him be praise for ever!

LETTER XVI.

Of Vows, and of the Dedicated Life in the World.

THE Counsel of Evangelical Obedience brings us to consider the question of vows; a question which, like many others, meets with somewhat rough handling in the present age, and chiefly from those who have never given the matter any serious consideration. This must not surprise us, for the things of God are spiritually discerned, and vows, inasmuch as they have to do with Him, have a divine character about them of which the world can know nothing. A vow is a promise made to God; it appeals to Him to witness its sincerity, and the violation of it involves the soul in the guilt of mortal sin. A rash vow is an insult to His most reverend Majesty, and it is far better not to vow, than to vow and not pay: hence the grave importance of understanding what constitutes the right matter for a vow, and under what circumstances vows ought or ought not to be taken.

Every Christian is bound by his baptismal covenant to the fulfilment of his baptismal vows, viz., of repentance, faith, and obedience to the moral law of God; but some Christians are called to a vowed life of stricter and more special obligations. The married are vowed to mutual love and fidelity, as representing the union that is betwixt Christ and the Church; the priest is bound by his ordination vows to yield canonical obedience to his ordinary; the religious is vowed to obedience to his superior and to stability in his society; and the dedicated soul in the world is vowed to the religious observance of one or more of the Evangelical Counsels.

Vows of this kind, taken by people in the world, are quite as truly vows, and are altogether as binding upon those who take them, as are the vows of religious in communities:

the difference simply being that, whereas the private vow is only a spiritual and moral act, the community vow is also an ecclesiastical act. The dedicated virgin in the world who is unfaithful to her vow is as truly a spiritual adulteress, as the cloistered virgin who is unfaithful to hers; but the sin of the latter would be an ecclesiastical as well as a spiritual offence, which the sin of the former would not. Community vows are accepted by the bishop, or his representative, in the name of the Church; but, private vows are not thus accepted, though they should always be made to the bishop, or to some priest having power to act for him. It would be difficult to imagine a more deplorable state of things than would be likely to result from a private vow undertaken rashly, and on the sole responsibility of the individual. Great caution is also to be observed as to the society or community in which religious vows are made, and no such vows should ever be taken except in a society approved by the bishop of the diocese. Of course any number of individuals may choose to place themselves under a person whom they call their superior, and may even make vows in their self-constituted community. Such vows would be binding inasmuch as they are vows; but they would not be religious vows in the technical sense, nor would the persons professing them be religious, nor their superior be a representative of Jesus Christ. Such a community would probably be schismatical, and would certainly be uncanonical; for we must take as an axiom in everything affecting Church life that nothing can be thoroughly Catholic which is not canonical—*i.e.*, which is not approved either directly or indirectly by the bishop of the diocese. The religious superior, then, must be canonically appointed according to the constitution of the particular society, and with the approval of the bishop. No one should take this office to himself, and the head of an uncanonical community is practically a self-constituted head, and cannot, therefore, represent our Blessed Lord, Who says of the authority which He Himself exercises, I can of My Own Self do nothing. The canonically-appointed superior alone has power to act in Christ's Name and in His stead, representing Him to the community as the curate does to the parish, and the bishop to the diocese.

Vows may be either temporary or perpetual. Perpetual vows of poverty and obedience belong most suitably to the religious state, and could seldom be prudently undertaken by those living in the world. This, however, does not apply to Evangelical Chastity, which may with great edification be made the matter of a perpetual vow, even by persons who are not in the perfect state of religion. Such a vow, however, could only be wisely taken by those who have already been on probation under a temporary vow : for a perpetual vow of virginity or chastity is as indissoluble as the marriage bond itself, of which it is the mystical counterpart : and the soul which is thus espoused to Christ can no more be dispensed from the obligations of its vow, than a wife can be dispensed from fidelity to her husband. If we acknowledge any power on earth by which marriage can be annulled, the same power might dispense from a vow of perpetual chastity ; but if we believe the marriage bond to be morally indissoluble, the same must be said of the vow of chastity. To believe otherwise, would be to suppose that a vow made directly to God, is not as binding as one made to man.

Temporary vows are only binding for so long as they are taken: and they may or may not be subject to dispensation during that time. When, as sometimes happens, we hear of the marriage of one who has professed Evangelical Chastity, however sad the action may be from a spiritual point of view, it does not at all necessarily follow that the person is guilty of perjury, or of any *moral* offence whatsoever. But surely, the whole question of dispensations is one that betokens a sorrowful decadence of Christian love and zeal. What would be thought of the bride who on the eve of her marriage was anxious to secure the way for a possible future divorce? and why is the virgin who aspires to union with Jesus as her heavenly Spouse to be hindered from it by warnings about the difficulty of obtaining dispensations? Is it not the case, my sisters, that in these lax days we are ready enough to put our trust in any child of man, and that it is only when we come to have direct dealings with our most dear and blessed God that we must needs be on our guard? No wonder that our modern Christianity finds a ready acceptance from a sceptical world with which it has so much in common; but, oh! what a grief it must be to the angels; what an insult it offers to Jesus Christ!

What has been said about the indispensability of vows must not be taken as applying to all vows, but only to some. Vows that are expressed in terms which imply possible dispensation are clearly in their nature dispensable; but those that are made absolutely, irrevocably, and in perpetuity, inasmuch as they are moral acts, and are made directly to God, can only be dispensed by Him. It should, however, be borne in mind that vows taken in a canonical community have an ecclesiastical as well as moral character, *and in so far as they are ecclesiastical acts*, they may be dispensed by the bishop, and the religious thus dispensed would then be morally in the same position as one leading a dedicated life under vows in the world.

There are two ways by which persons living in the world may observe the Counsels of Perfection. The first is freely, with nothing more than an interior resolution to guide the individual conscience; the second is religiously, by means of vows. For as we have already seen, vows made to God, even by persons living in the world, are sometimes called religious, and are held to have something of the religious state, although not the perfect state of religion.* "Religion" means "binding," and therefore any person in so far as he is bound by vow to observe the Counsels, is, to that degree, and in that measure, "religious," and in "religion."

From the earliest times of Christianity, in all ages of the Church, and in every land, there have been found persons of both sexes who, while still living in the world, have bound themselves by vow to observe one or more of the Counsels of Perfection. This was notably the case during the times of persecution, previous to the formation of religious communities. Many suffered martyrdom rather than lose the virginal chastity in which they had consecrated themselves to Christ. Later on, when persecution ceased, the Church was free to erect monastic institutions, and to develop the religious life, the foundations of which had been already laid by the fathers of the desert; but neither then, nor at any later period, has the monastic state been the only one in which Christians have been free to dedicate them-

* Suarez: "The Religious State." Most of the statements made in this letter are from the same author.

selves by vow to the observance of the Evangelical Counsels. The Church has never denied this privilege to any of her children who believe themselves thus called of God ; on the contrary, a very slight acquaintance with her history is enough to shew that she upholds and approves it. To vow any better thing to God, out of love to Him and desire for His glory, is in itself clearly a good and wholesome act. To serve Him under a vow, denying ourselves voluntarily a thing which we might lawfully enjoy, is in itself nobler than the same service offered without any vow. Those to whom God has given this blessed vocation assure us that there is no greater safeguard, and no truer joy, than a life thus separated and consecrated to Him.

But what is best in itself is not always best for every individual, and the grace of God often leads souls to the highest degree of perfection by what is not in itself the most perfect way. We must remember, too, that this is a question of vocation, and we cannot call ourselves to a vowed life in the world any more than we can call ourselves to the cloister. For a vowed life places us, if not visibly, yet invisibly, in another order of things. In the sight of men we may be the same, but before God and His saints and angels we are different. We have new temptations to resist, new foes to fight, new hardships to endure, new perils to undergo. Supernaturally our circumstances have changed. Some things which used to be lawful for us would now be mortal sin, and we can sin venially with a fearful ease, where souls not thus bound could not possibly sin at all. Vows to observe the Counsels of Perfection, whether made in the world or in the cloister, bring the soul into a special relation towards God. They place it in the light of His Perfection, and keep it there. It sees and hears sights and sounds which until now it has not known. In the cloister all hindrances to holiness are, as far as possible, removed, that the religious may be free to attend to the things of God without distraction. In the world no hindrances are removed, yet the vowed soul is as truly bound to aim at perfection as the most enclosed religious. We should be very rash if we sought this thing for ourselves. It must be God's choice for us, for only those whom He calls to this way can hope to persevere. The difficulties and dangers are so many and so great, that some will have it that in the present state of the Church and of society, such vows ought not to be taken by persons living in the world. But where God gives the vocation He will also give the grace; and where vocation is given, let us remember, no *choice* can possibly remain to the obedient soul.

Looking at the question in the abstract, there does not seem any reason why Christians should not be as free now as in every other age, to dedicate themselves by vow to God. We claim a marvellous liberty in all things but in His service. We stand by every right but our right of serving Him. We may devote ourselves to anything else that we please; literature, science, art, fashion, pleasure, all have their votaries. No one finds fault with a person who spends half his days in amusement, but what would be said of one who spent half of them in prayer? People are ready enough to risk their health in pleasure, are they equally willing to risk it in devotion? There are many who make themselves martyrs to fashion; are there any of whom it can be said that they lay down their lives for Jesus?

Yes, my sisters, thank God, there are. We may not know them, but He does. Their virgin names are written in the Lamb's

Book of Life, and in the day when that Book is opened they will be found among those who are worthy. In the present age, as in every other, the Catholic Church recognizes and honours the vocation to an uncloistered virgin life. Many, very many, of our Christian sisters all over the world, whom God has not called into communities, are leading vowed and dedicated lives in their own secular homes; they are witnesses to Christ, they testify of Jesus, the savour of His good ointments is upon them, and, in spite of itself, the world owns their influence.* If persecution were to arise, they would die rather than lose their virginity. They despise all things for the love of Jesus, their Lord, to Whom alone they have vowed themselves as the Bridegroom of their souls. While they witness to Christ in the world they labour for Him in His Church. They serve the Lord with fastings and prayers, or they give themselves to active works of charity among their neighbours; they keep themselves unspotted in the midst of defilement, and reflect the purity of Jesus and

* These, in earlier ages known as "nuns" came afterwards to be called "Devotes;" in Italy, "Beatas."

cause His light to shine in dark places, and win souls to Christ by their simple likeness to Him. Such was Victorine de Galard Terraube, who lived a dedicated virgin life in the midst of French society in the early part of the present century, a record of which has been given to us in Lady Herbert's well-known book, "Three Phases of Christian Love." Such, in our own days, was the gentle author of "Le Vol d'une Ame," a book which perhaps would have been better unpublished, since it clearly was never meant for general criticism. Such again was Maria Franchi de Cavalieri, a young girl of noble birth and remarkable holiness, "whose virgin heart," to use the words of her biographer, was "free from earthly attachment," and whose chief longing was "to emulate even in the world, the perfection of convent life." She was hindered (probably through ill-health) from entering a community; but shortly before her death, in 1888, at the early age of twenty-five, she made her vows to her spiritual father, as had long been her earnest desire. It would be easy to mention others, but these will be enough to shew that the vocation of which we are speaking is not a mere romance of past ages, but a power in the present day.

And if it be objected, as it most surely will, that the examples quoted are none of them those of our own countrywomen, that is an argument that will hardly carry weight if we really believe in our Catholicism. Are English maidens less free to devote themselves exclusively to Jesus than the maidens of Italy or France? Is our country, once the island of saints, to yield henceforth no harvest of virgin souls to God? Is the mere fact of our nationality enough to put a barrier between us and Him? Uncloistered virginity is recognized as a distinct vocation in other lands, but with us it is not so, and those whose care it should be to defend its sacred rights, for the most part either condemn or ignore it. But if we are truly Catholic, and if we make our special appeal to primitive Christianity, it is difficult to see on what ground we are forbidden to consecrate and vow our virgin life to God. Holy virginity was one of the chief glories of the early Church, and if we in England are to be truly primitive and apostolic, as well as Catholic, this development of the Christian life must surely be allowed to us.

But, we are told, times have altered; circumstances have changed; things are not as they were so many centuries ago. In some ways this is quite true, but not, I think, as regards the question before us. The love of holy virginity, a dedicated virgin life, simply means *an exclusive devotion to Jesus.* It meant this in the first century, and it means the same now. Where, then, is the difference? Has Jesus altered? He is the Unchangeable God. Has the Church altered? She is unchangeable, like her Lord. Has the world altered? It hates Jesus and His Church as much as ever. Now, as truly as in apostolic times, "all that will live godly in Christ Jesus *must* suffer persecution;" to *devote* oneself to Him is not easier now than it was then. On the contrary, the world wears such a look of innocence that it is more seductive than ever. Fashion knows how to seem religious, and pleasure can put on such an artful appearance of duty, that it is often very difficult to know right from wrong, or to distinguish between truth and falsehood. If ever something were needed to impart spiritual stability to souls living in the world it is needed now, for an age of luxury and comfort makes devotion to the Crucified no easy thing. Perhaps, when we consider the matter from this point of view, we shall see that vows, however out of harmony they may be with the spirit of the age, are not on that account less in keeping with the spirit of that Church which is the same in all ages, and to which we belong.

So then, dear sisters, let us plead our cause with God. To us, under Him, may belong the glory of claiming this, our true woman's right ; and not only of claiming it, but of securing it. Let us ask Him to plead it for us with those who strive with us, whether in the world or in the Church ; and let us plead it ourselves in silence, and with tears. We cannot teach our teachers, but we can pray that they may be illuminated to recognize our vocation and its needs. Meanwhile, if not permitted to dedicate our virgin life to Him by vow, we may separate ourselves in will and purpose unto Him. If we may not yet pledge ourselves to Him with our lips, we may do so in our heart, and until we are free to utter it that will suffice, for if only we are faithful to present grace we may be sure of future guidance.

We have spoken thus far of the vow of chastity. This is the Counsel most generally observed in the world: it is perhaps the most attractive in itself, as arising from the personal love of our divine Lord, and it is also the most practically possible. It involves the individual in fewer complications than the other Counsels, and adapts itself to a greater variety of circumstances. But it generally leads on to the observance in a greater or less degree of the Counsels of obedience and poverty, both of which, under fitting circumstances, may be made the matter of a vow. Very little need be said about this here. A vow of obedience, taken in the world, would necessarily be with limitations, and should be made with the utmost discretion. It is open to so much possible danger, and might prove such a fatal snare to the soul, that it is often condemned altogether, even by those who allow the vow of chastity. But in spite of all that can be said against it, so great an authority as the devout and learned Suarez approves it in particular cases.

Speaking generally, the vow of poverty can even less suitably be made by persons living in the world. It would result in very practical difficulties, and might even hinder, rather than help, perfection. The spirit of poverty, detachment, may be most eminently attained in the world ; but, in so far as it is matter of vow, poverty may be said to belong almost exclusively to the religious state.

"Where the spirit of the Lord is, there is liberty." Unless the bondage of vows is found to be a most true and blessed freedom, they cannot be God's Will for any soul. Vows certainly demand a sacrifice, but those who are called to make them say that it is a sacrifice of joy. The sufferings in which they involve the soul are its road to glory, the temptations which they attract to it are the measure of its blessedness. Yet perhaps they are not meant for us, nor we for them. We need not on that account lose heart. God is our End; that is enough. Let Him choose the way we shall take to come to Him. It cannot disappoint us. We have only to make His choice our own, and we shall find ourselves in the haven of our desire, at peace, and in union with Him.

But let us remind ourselves once more what such a life of dedication means. It means that we commit ourselves to the complete fulfilment of the whole Gospel code. It means that the cross is to be branded, as with living fire, upon every detail of our life, until our whole self is crucified. It means that we are to be dead, and our life hid with Christ in God. In the midst of the world we are to be separate, consecrate, apart, having nothing in common with its wisdom, its pleasures, its wealth : our possessions laid at the feet of Jesus, our hearts united with His Heart, our wills surrendered to His Will; poor, yet having all things; virgins, yet most truly brides; bond-servants, yet free indeed. For us, no surrender, no compromise, no coming to terms with the world, can ever be possible. When the world speaks we shall pay no heed to it, listening only to Christ's, " But *I* say unto you." When the world sneers we shall rejoice, for did it not mock Him ? When it persecutes we shall be glad, for did it not seek to destroy Him ? When it condemns we shall possess our souls in peace, for did it not reckon Him among the transgressors ? Truth came, and spoke to the world, and it said of Him, " He blasphemeth." Light came and shined in the world, and it loved the darkness best. Purity came, and trod with unspotted foot through the defilement of the world, and it said of Him, " He hath a devil." Mercy came to judge the world in righteousness, and it declared Him to be guilty of death. Love came and broke His Heart, and died to save the world, and the world spoke of Him then, and speaks of Him even yet, as "that deceiver." And we are called with a special vocation to follow Him, that, as He is, so we may be in this world; reviled, rejected, scorned, the spouses in very truth of a Crucified God.

. Clearly, then, perfection is no easy thing. We cannot slip into it, we must toil into it. Unless we are desperately in earnest we shall never attain to it, and if we are in earnest it will cost us our life. In responding to the call we rise and follow Jesus; and where does He go, but to Calvary? We take up the cross, and we know what that means,—henceforth we are alway delivered unto death for Jesus' sake. This is to be our dedication. The world scorns it. Of course it does. Our friends resent it. Of course they do. The devil persecutes us for it, the flesh cries out against it; but the voice of Jesus has spoken in our heart, and to us His "Follow Me" means this, and nothing less than this, nor would we for the whole world be saved one grief of our passion, or spared one thorn from our crown.

Yet, high as our vocation is, let us never forget that the dedicated life has it own special danger, the temptation to spiritual pride. If, dearest sisters, we would be truly the virgin-spouses of Christ, we must keep ourselves very humble indeed. For lack of this humility there have been not unknown to the Church, virgins whose lives were a scandal not only to the Christian profession, but to very womanhood. This was notoriously the case in the North African Church in the third century, of whose virgins we read that "some were petulant in behaviour and immodest in attire. So far from veiling themselves from the gaze of a profane world, according to the strict notions of Tertullian, they seemed to have been living almost without rule. They wasted their time; they spent their money capriciously; they dressed and painted to such excess that, when God looked for the faces of His elect, He saw only the false colours and gewgaws of the devil. Others of them became notorious as gossips. They were wont to gad about from house to house; and delighted in the wanton merry-makings which African society tolerated and encouraged at marriage feasts. Some preferred the heathen to the Christian rule of decency, and did not scruple to be seen amongst the unblushing rabble of both sexes that frequented the public baths. Their manners, in short, were not only scandalous, but —from a modern point of view, and without reference to the omnipotence of fashion in determining questions of decorum — they might be thought inconsistent with any sense at all of Christian obligations." And the explanation of this state of things seems to have been that "the virgins, regarded more and more as the flower of Christianity, and treated for that reason with a perilous indulgence—were not a little crazed by the flattery, which even the Bishops, when they ventured to reprove them, could not prudently withhold."*

It is not likely at present that the high esteem shown towards us by our ecclesiastical superiors will be sufficient to turn our heads ; but our peril will be quite as great. if we at all highly esteem ourselves. Spiritual pride is the sure precursor of a lax morality. So then, let us, who think that we stand, take heed lest we fall. Like the Blessed Mary, the highest and the lowliest of all God's creatures, let us veil ourselves

* Mahan's Church History, Bk. ii. ch. 2.

in silence and in secresy from the gaze of men ; and, since our lot is cast in the world, let us remain as much as possible in the retreat of our own homes, and when duty takes us elsewhere let us make to ourselves "a little grating of the fear of God," and so contrive to live unnoticed and unknown, save to the angels and to Him. Above all, let us beware of ever talking about our own spiritual experiences, unless it is our positive duty to do so, and then let it be only to those whose aim is one with our own. When Joseph unwisely made confidants of his brethren, and told them of his mysterious dreams, the only effect that it had upon them was to make them angry, "Behold this dreamer cometh," they said, and, moved with envy, they sold him to be a bond-servant. Let us take warning from this example, and observe a prudent silence in all matters concerning the interior life. Our Blessed Lady, when she was "found with child of the Holy Ghost," was content to be misunderstood and suspected even by her espoused husband. She did not open her lips in her own defence, she committed her cause to God, and left it to Him to vindicate her spotless virginal purity, and to reveal also to

St. Joseph the mystery of her divine maternity. She did not breathe a word of her joy even to Elizabeth, until the Holy Ghost Himself inspired her heavenly Magnificat. "My secret to myself" has ever been the motto of the saints : let it be ours too, and even though it may not make us all that they were, it will save us from many an unworthiness, and will help to hide us into closer union with Him Who was in the world, and the world knew Him not, and Who has called us to be as He is.

Now unto Him that is able to do exceeding abundantly above all that we ask or think, according to the power that worketh in us, unto Him be glory.

LETTER XVII.

Of Special Devotions.

ONE of the greatest helps we can possibly have, my sisters, in the practice of Evangelical Perfection, is the grace of a special devotion. I call it a grace, because it is something which we cannot arrive at by any natural process. It consists in a divine attraction to some particular point or mystery of our holy faith, by means of which the soul receives a definite spiritual character, a Christ-likeness peculiar to itself. Thus, to a certain extent, special devotion does for the individual, what the spirit of the society does for a community, and for those who are living in the world it would be difficult to exaggerate its importance. Without it, the practice of perfection is almost sure to languish, if not to fail altogether, but with it the whole spiritual life gathers tone and strength ; and perseverance, though not ensured, is immensely helped. Our minds are so small, and God's truth is so great, that it is quite beyond our power in this life fully to grasp and assimilate into ourselves all the various mysteries which the faith presents to us : the whole realm of revelation is too vast to be traversed in time, and, thank God, we have eternity to do it in. Just as in the natural sciences there are classifications of subjects, and departments of knowledge, each supplying a distinct branch of study, and intellectual food for a lifetime, so with theology, which is the science of God, it is divided and sub-divided into different mysteries, each of which, while intimately connected with all the others, may be considered separately and by itself. In the study of science different minds are differently attracted; one man is drawn to geology as his special subject, another to botany, a third lives among the stars, while a fourth retires into the invisible regions of mathematics, and a fifth into the still more abstruse realms of music. No one pretends to a complete knowledge of any of these sciences; still less would he dream of aspiring to a universal knowledge of every science. The wisest student is ever the most conscious of his own ignorance, and the deepest scholar is the most truly humble. If such is the case with merely human learning, what shall we say of that which is divine? The science which treats of the mysteries of the faith is theology, and the proper subject of theology is God. Theology, therefore, treats of the Infinite; and it stands to reason that finite minds can only consider it in detail, by degrees, and in succession. These details, these degrees, and this succession, supply the subjects for special devotion. Special devotion helps us, as it were, to examine in detail the great temple of Catholic truth. There is the sanctuary of the Being of God, the doctrine of the Most Holy Trinity, with its Threefold Personality, and Unity of Essence, the Life that is Love, Begetting, Begotten, and Proceeding. In this Life are also contained those mysterious depths, which, for lack of words, we name the Attributes or Perfections of God, each of which supplies a subject for special devotion. Thus, there may be a devotion either to the mystery of the Blessed Trinity in Unity, or to the consideration of God as He is in Himself,—Love, Holiness, Omniscience, Omnipresence, Immutability, Truth, Beauty, Magnificence; or as He reveals Himself to His creatures, in Patience, Strength, Mercy, Justice, Providence. Our Blessed Lord says, "No man cometh unto the Father but by Me," and all special devotion to the Most Holy Trinity, or to the divine Attributes, is the growth and outcome of devotion to the Person of Christ, Incarnate God. The Incarnation, therefore, is the root mystery of every special devotion that is really Catholic, and that will bear the strain of use; for a devotion that is not practical is sure not to be quite Catholic, and what is uncatholic can never be sanctifying. We must be careful not to try and give ourselves a special devotion; still more we must avoid any attempt to invent one for ourselves. Nothing that does not distinctly bear upon it the sign royal of the Incarnation, nothing that does not come to us through the knowledge of Jesus, God and Man, can be a proper subject for devotion.

The Incarnate Life supplies abundant matter for the contemplation of devout souls, and the attraction is generally at first given to a mystery with which we already seem to be familiar. But when we come to apply ourselves to it we find out its hidden beauties, and the longer we study them, the more fully they unfold themselves to us, so that each new beauty of the mystery seems to contain fresh beauties within itself, and every one of these is like a distinct revelation of God. This is especially true of the mysteries of the Incarnate Life. Our Lord's immaculate Conception and His spotless Birth, the Sacred Infancy, the Holy Childhood, His Youth, His Hidden Life, and His active Ministry, each contains a world of wonders within itself, which it would need many life-times to explore, and many hearts to love with, before it could be at all duly honoured. The Passion is a subject that is simply inexhaustible. Saints have fed upon it for nearly nineteen centuries, and it is still as fresh as ever. "I, if I be lifted up," said Christ, "will draw all men unto Me." It may be considered either in itself, as culminating in the Crucifix, or in any one of its countless details, or under any of its most striking aspects, such, for example, as the Precious Blood, the Five Wounds, or the Holy Cross. The Risen Life during the great Forty Days suggests an intensely spiritual devotion, as do also the Ascension, and the Mediatorial Life of our glorified Lord. The Blessed Sacrament seems to gather up into itself all the particular mysteries of the Incarnate Life, and presents them to the eye of faith successively, according to the Church's seasons, and always under new aspects.

Devotion to the Sacred Heart has a peculiar attraction for dedicated souls, and for those whom God trains for Himself through much sorrow; and perhaps it is the most satisfying of all special devotions, being, as it is, so intimately connected with devotion to the most Holy Trinity, and in its very nature, as resulting from the Hypostatic Union, inexhaustible. Nevertheless, this devotion is one about which sad misunderstandings exist, and for that reason we shall do well to go into it a little more fully. We not unfrequently hear most shocking things said about devotion to the Sacred Heart, even by those who really love our Lord; and there is, alas! too reasonable a foundation for some things which are thus said; for it cannot be denied that a particular form of this devotion does exist, which must appear at least irreverent to any thoughtful mind. No doubt, this devotion, like every other that is connected with the Incarnation, has its physical side, but that is not the side to be chiefly thought of and dwelt upon.

What then, we may ask, *is* devotion to the Sacred Heart? It is a devotion to the interior life of Jesus, resulting in an intimate knowledge of His feelings, a sharing of His tastes, a sympathy with His interests, an intuitive perception of even His unexpressed wishes. A child of the Sacred Heart not only loves what Jesus loves, and hates what He hates, but also strives to love in the way that Jesus loves, and to hate in the way He hates. Devotion to the Heart of Jesus is only a new name for a devotion that is as old as Christianity itself. It was this, the special devotion of the Apostolic Church, that St. Paul so earnestly desired to see in his spiritual children at Philippi, when he said, "Let this mind be in you which was also in Christ Jesus;" and that made him exclaim exultingly to his Corinthian converts, "We have the mind of Christ." It forms the soul on the model of the interior spirit of Jesus, or rather it tends to raise the soul to such perfection, that Christ Himself is formed in it. Again, you see, I am quoting St. Paul, and indeed there is no such manual of the Sacred Heart as the Book of the divine Scriptures, whether we turn to the Law, the Psalms, or the Prophets of the Old and New Testaments; "for they are they," saith Jesus, "which testify of Me."

The component parts of this devotion are adoration, reparation, and intercession, which summarize, so to speak, the interior acts of the whole Incarnate Life, and exhibit to us the chief characteristics of our Lord's own personal piety. If only this devotion, thus understood, were more common among us, what a tremendous power it would be! What marvels of grace would be taking place every day, what heroic ventures of faith, what generous enterprizes of charity!

How we should spend ourselves for God, and in how rich a harvest would the Catholic Church rejoice. This, let us be sure, is the true meaning of devotion to the Sacred Heart, as a very slight acquaintance with foreign devotional literature is sufficient to shew.

Special devotion to the Holy Ghost needs to be carefully guarded, otherwise it tends to divide the Unity of Substance in the Godhead. Particular devotion to any Person of the Trinity *in Himself, as a distinct Person*, is uncatholic. Thus, special devotion to the Eternal Son, except as Jesus, Incarnate God, would be heretical, and so also would special devotion to the Holy Ghost, except as the Comforter, the Paraclete, by which name is declared His mission to man, and His office in the Church, the Mystical Body of Christ. This goes to support what has already been said, that nothing is an orthodox subject for special devotion unless supplied by the root doctrine of the Incarnation. " The Comforter shall take *of Mine*," says Christ, "He shall testify *of Me*." The Holy Ghost was not given till Jesus was glorified. Keeping this in view, special devotion to the Holy Ghost is most sanctifying, but we cannot be specially devoted to Him as He is in Himself, God, for that at once makes an inequality in the Godhead which is "all One." In these days, when stress is sometimes laid upon the "cultus of the Holy Ghost," we must be careful to remember this. Let those who are attracted to this devotion specially honour Him as the Comforting, Sanctifying, Informing Spirit, the Spirit of Jesus, for in no other way can He rightly be *specially* honoured.

The Incarnation is not only the way to God, it is the way, the only true way, to all science, whether of nature or of grace. Everything that is, exists because of God, it represents an eternal thought of His Mind, which He has given expression to, and projected from Himself, in the act of creating. All that God has made is, like Himself, very good, and all that He has redeemed from sin, and sanctified, partakes of His Divine Nature. "Ye are gods, and ye are all the children of the Most Highest." The Incarnation leads us up to the uncreated life of God, and shows us God as He is in Himself; it also leads us out into the created Life of God, and shows Him to us as He is in His creatures. What a field for special devotion this presents to us. The whole earth is full of His goodness; His way is in the sea, and His strength in the hills. He causes His voice to be heard from heaven, and shines in lightning on the ground; He makes the clouds His chariot, and walks upon the wind, and clothes Himself with light, and dwells in the thick darkness. Everything testifies of Him, not only as Creator, but as Redeemer too. He teaches the birds to make the sign of the cross as they spread their wings, and tips the daisies with red, thereby reminding us of the Precious Blood; and puts the seal of His Passion on all suffering, and yet fills the world with gladness, because of His own great joy. If only we believed in grace half as much as we do in nature, what revelations of God we should always be having! In His Light we should see light, and all light would be His. Nothing would perplex us, for He is the explanation of all mystery; nothing could be exaggerated, for we should see in Him the proportion of the Faith. We should share His Mind about everything, and honour Him in all, as He honours Himself. Devotion to our Blessed Lady, formed on this basis, would be a most divine thing, for we should be doing exactly what God does, neither more nor less, and magnifying her, not for any merits of her own, but for His grace in her whom He makes to be full of grace.

So, too, of devotion to the saints and angels. God loves Himself in all; let us love Him in them, praise Him in them, rejoice in Him in them, and our devotion to them will be not only very simple and practical, but very heavenly too, for it will be God's own devotion, His devotion to Himself, not as He exists essentially in Himself uncreated, but as He exists accidentally outside Himself, in creation.

Let us make much, dear sisters, of any attraction which we are conscious of in the spiritual life, for most surely the Holy Ghost has given it for a special purpose, and intends that we should use it as a means to sanctification. Let us cultivate the devotion towards which we are chiefly drawn, and so grow into the spirit of some one at least of the mysteries of God. It will give tone to our character, and help to form in us an interior atmosphere, wherein the graces that we most need will grow and mature. If we are to serve God in the world it will help to keep us separate from it, by giving us a divine and hidden spirit; while if we are preparing for the religious state it will help us to be patient, while it quickens our desire. Only, let us remember that we cannot give ourselves a special devotion, any more than we can give ourselves a vocation, and if we are not conscious as yet of any particular attraction let us seek it in prayer, and ask counsel of our director.

Our special devotion may not be always the same; "the wind bloweth where it listeth," and the Holy Spirit frequently leads a soul to venerate different mysteries successively, or even several at once. Devotion to any mystery of our Lord's Incarnate Life may safely be practised as the basis upon which a whole character may be formed, but this is hardly the case with devotion to the divine Attributes, which cannot be really considered by the human mind except as revealed in the Person of Jesus Christ. No devotion to angels and saints, nor even to the Blessed Mother of God, could safely exist at all, except in subordination to a higher devotion, and if made the sole basis of the interior life would most surely be misleading. For the End of our being is God in Himself, as revealed to us in the Person of Jesus Christ, and not as He is pleased to manifest Himself otherwise. Our lives are to be formed in the spirit of Jesus, till He Himself be formed in us. Let "Jesus only" be our motto, and then we may fearlessly yield ourselves to follow any attraction which the Holy Ghost may give us.

Our Lord's own special devotion was to the Will of God. It was His Blessed Mother's too; hers, because His. It would be interesting and delightful to trace out what might seem to have been the particular attraction of many of the saints, both in the Old and New Testaments; but it would perhaps be thought fanciful. What is more important is that we should know what is our own, and that we should be faithful to its grace. It is of more vital importance to us, and will more affect our eternity, than any mere outward circumstances of our life. It is bound up with our predestination, which is the glory of God, and is intended to develop in us that heavenly character by which our Lord will recognise us at the last as belonging to Himself.

Here, my sisters, I will end these instructions. They are mere outlines—nothing more—of what souls dedicated to the Life of the Counsels in the world should try to aim at. The lessons which they contain are, with few exceptions, the result of observation or of experience, and, with the guidance of the Holy Spirit, you will be able to supply for yourselves things which I have purposely, or ignorantly, omitted ; while, in return for the slight effort which I have been allowed to make on your behalf, I beg you, as you close this book to ask God to bless it both to you and to me.

May the very God of peace sanctify you wholly, and I pray God that your whole spirit and soul and body be preserved blameless unto the coming of our Lord Jesus Christ. Faithful is He that calleth you, Who also will do it.

Glory be to the Father, and to the Son : and to the Holy Ghost.

As it was in the beginning, is now, and ever shall be : world without end. Amen.

A RULE OF LIFE.†

The following is intended only as offering suggestions to those who may find difficulty in making a rule for themselves. Certain things which might well be practised by some persons, but which would be unsuitable for others, are marked (*). It is generally better to find out by experience whether a particular practice is edifying to ourselves personally, before pledging ourselves to observe it as part of our rule; and we must be careful never to do anything which would be a needless aggravation to other people.

In the Name of the Father, and of the Son, and of the Holy Ghost. Amen.

I, *N.*, resolve by the grace of God, and with the counsel of my spiritual father, to devote myself henceforth to the service of Jesus Christ, as a religious accidentally obliged to live in the world, observing the Counsels of Perfection (so far as my state allows), in the following ways :—

I. *Poverty : Exterior.* By never spending money on my own pleasure, nor for my own comfort, except health require it ; and by using all that I have as belonging to God, and as having no rights over it except for His glory.

By spending with an interior motive of charity all that has to be spent on things which are not in them-

† By permission.

selves distinctly charity, *e.g.* to please others, or to avoid being thought mortified.

By dressing as simply as I may ;* always in dark colours ;* avoiding rich materials, unnecessary ornaments and jewels. Avoiding also, on the other hand, singularity, untidiness and shabbiness in attire, as not likely in my case to tend to humility.

By practising economy wherever I can (even in such things as matches and note-paper) but unaffectedly.

By retaining as few personal possessions as possible, and by regarding these as only mine in the using.

By generosity in lending ; especially books, and those things which I should most regret the loss of.

By never contending for my own personal rights.

Poverty : Interior. By never talking about myself if I can possibly help it, even indirectly, or to my own discredit.

By avoiding praise, and by doing some definite act of bodily penance when I fall into the snare of seeking it ; (or, if this should not be permitted, to kiss the crucifix, by way of reparation for having so detracted from the glory of God).

By willingly being ignored, and cheerfully accepting humiliations—*e.g.* being thought incapable of doing things that I know quite well how to do ; having my word doubted, &c.

By using those things which most hurt my pride, as special means of union with our Lord.

By putting others forward, and taking the last place myself.

By rejoicing in the greater gifts of others, whereby they are able to serve God better than I.

By humility of mind, showing itself in respect and reverence for the opinions and feelings of others.

A RULE OF LIFE. 251

II. *Chastity: Exterior.* By aiming at a perfect discipline of all my senses ; of *sight*, by not allowing myself to look at artistic objects of a secular kind unless duty or charity demand it; carefully guarding my eyes, and never allowing them to rest on anything out of mere curiosity ; not looking into shop windows when alone ; not reading street or *newspaper advertisements ; not stopping, nor turning to look at any unusual sights ; not noticing other people's dress ; not looking out of the window at passing objects.

By discipline of the sense of *hearing* : not listening by choice to secular conversation, music, or songs ; if obliged to do so, and I find it distasteful, to accept this as the discipline, and to take part in everything of the kind quite as if I enjoyed it ; if, on the other hand, I find an innocent pleasure in it, to offer this with thanksgiving to the Giver of all good things. Mortifying my natural curiosity to hear news ; listening kindly and sympathetically to those whose conversation is uninteresting to me ; but never taking part in uncharitable conversation, nor willingly hearing it ; and never tolerating for a moment any that is in the least unchaste. Never listening to flattery if I can help it, and doing some definite act of (bodily) penance when I fall into this snare.

By discipline of the sense of *taste ;* eating what is set before me, whether I like it or not, and never leaving any food on my plate ; when I have the choice, choosing those things which I like least, if I can do so without being noticed ; denying myself in some special way on days of abstinence, over and above what is commanded by the Church ; never eating or drinking except at meals, unless duty or charity demand it.

By discipline of the sense of *touch;* avoiding, as far as possible, soft underclothing, soft beds, pillows, easy chairs, and self-indulgent attitudes; observing a perfect modesty in all my actions, when alone as much as when with others. * Not allowing myself to be touched familiarly, nor to receive caresses from anyone, even of my own sex. (If obliged to accept such, to offer it as an act of union with Jesus in His Passion.)

By discipline of the sense of *smell*; never using artificial perfumes; nor complaining of unpleasant smells, unless I believe them to be injurious to health.

By discipline of speech; observing silence before Mass and Communion,* and on my way to and from Confession. At other times, speaking as little as duty and charity permit; never interrupting others in conversation, but willingly allowing myself to be interrupted. Never expressing an opinion except with charity and modesty. Avoiding anything like slang, or grotesque jests or expressions; speaking gently, but without affectation; always with grace, in honour of Christ *the Word.*

By discipline of manner; not laughing noisily; shewing reverence in all my actions, as mindful of the Presence of God; moving about quietly, avoiding hurry, excitement, and gesticulation.

By not going into company more than my duty absolutely requires; * nor to entertainments of any kind, above all, not to the theatre. † If obliged to go, out of deference to the wishes of *parents or guardians,* to do so with a good grace, offering it to Jesus as an act of obedience, and thus using it as a means of glorifying God.

Chastity : Interior.—By discipline of the affections;

† It may be questioned whether any others have a right to command us in these matters.

not allowing myself to rest in the love or sympathy of any creature, but to love all in and for God. Putting away, at whatever cost to myself, all merely natural friendships : not allowing myself to regard anyone or anything as essential to my happiness or to my perfection.

By discipline of the desires ; not wishing anything for myself that God does not wish for me, and that only in the degree which He desires it, and for the object for which He desires it ; His glory, not my sanctification, the End of my being.

By discipline of the thoughts ; not allowing my mind to dwell for a moment upon anything which I could not acceptably offer to Jesus.

By purity of intention ; doing all things to the glory of God, and thus sanctifying my commonest actions.

III. *Obedience : Exterior.*—By punctuality in rising and * retiring, and in keeping household rules and hours. † By keeping a time-table if possible. By not allowing work to interfere with devotion, nor devotion with work.

By shewing respect and courtesy to everyone, especially to those with whom I live ; and to servants, never giving an order except in the form of a request.

By cheerfully accepting the discipline of domestic life, using it as a means of sanctification, just as a religious should accept the discipline of community life.

By never complaining of the weather, nor of trifling bodily ailments ; nor of having to wait for anything ; nor of fatigue, discomfort, &c.

By accepting exterior distractions, *e.g.*, interrup-

† As a matter of fact this is very seldom possible.

tions to work, devotions, &c., as a true discipline of my will, and therefore as means of conforming me to the likeness of Christ.

By gladly doing for others the lowliest offices.

*By doing every day some menial work, in honour of our Lord's hidden Life.

Obedience: Interior.—By an absolute surrender of myself to God, to follow His leading, and to do His will in all things.

By an unquestioning and whole-hearted submission to my director in all things affecting my vocation, my rule, and my work for God.

By readily yielding to the wishes of others, even against my own judgment (except when I myself am the one in authority), in all things not opposed to the Will of God, the counsel of my director, and this rule.

By a peaceful acceptance of secret trials, especially those which come to me through others not recognising my vocation, or resenting it if known.

As to mortification. Using such bodily austerities as may be allowed me by my director, and observing in all these things perseverance, humility, and discretion.

As to devotion. Setting apart a definite time every day for prayer and spiritual reading.

†Assisting at Mass every day, if possible.

Confessing and communicating as often as allowed by my director; and never making extra Communions without leave.

Honouring with special devotion, in order to practical holiness of life . . . . (*the particular mysteries and saints to which I feel myself divinely attracted*).

† For most people a little fresh air and exercise before breakfast is the best of all tonics.

A RULE OF LIFE, ETC. 255

*Making, if possible, a monthly day's retreat, and an annual retreat of three days or longer.

By means of this rule I desire to keep myself unspotted from the world, and to live only for God and His glory, as separated by a special dedication to His service in the state of holy virginity, to which He has called me.
So help me God, by His Holy Spirit, through Jesus Christ our Lord.

(Signed)

Those who desire solitude, yet whose duty keeps them in the world, would do well to follow the example of the saints who, under like circumstances, made a home in their hearts for Jesus, a little oratory into which they may always retreat, and be alone with Him. The following lines suggest a method in which this may be done.

Chapel of Ease.

I build within my soul a shrine apart,
And consecrate it to the Sacred Heart ;
An altar in the midst thereof I raise,
And offer there the Sacrifice of praise ;
Above it the sweet Cross of Christ I sign,
And burn before it love's red lamp divine ;
Curtains on either side of this I draw,
And call them holy Fear, and loving Awe,
Twin candles on my altar you may see,
Their names are Patience and Humility,
But though these taper lights I hourly trim,
They gutter sadly, and their flame goes dim.

So then, to keep my sanctuary bright,
I offer virgin-lilies pure and white;
The which I know my Lord will surely take
For His own pureness', and our Lady's, sake.
Then, while their fragrance sweetens all the air,
I add thereto the frankincense of prayer.
My song and music are soft monotone,
The Name of Jesus, and the Spirit's moan.
Three times a day I ring my Ave bell,
And say "Hail Mary" with St. Gabriel.
The Master teacheth me to say my beads,
Full well He knoweth His poor scholar's needs:
My patron saints do here converse with me,
And my good angel keeps me company;
And so, when other things do me displease,
I to my chapel go, and there find ease.

www.ingramcontent.com/pod-product-compliance
Lightning Source LLC
Chambersburg PA
CBHW032137230426
43672CB00011B/2369